Waking Up Blind: Lawsuits Over Eye Surgery

Waking Up Blind: Lawsuits Over Eye Surgery

By Tom Harbin, M.D.

LANGDON STREET PRESS

Langdon Street Press
212 3rd Avenue North, Suite 290
Minneapolis, MN 55401
612.455.2293
www.langdonstreetpress.com

ISBN - 978-1-934938-87-4
ISBN - 1-934938-87-4
LCCN - 2009934753

Book sales for North America and international:
Itasca Books, 3501 Highway 100 South, Suite 220
Minneapolis, MN 55416
Phone: 952.345.4488 (toll free 1.800.901.3480)
Fax: 952.920.0541; email to orders@itascabooks.com

Typeset by Peggy LeTrent

Printed in the United States of America

Author's note: The events described herein are true and occurred between 1976 and 1997. Because I necessarily introduce many names, I provide a list of the participants after the epilogue so the reader can avoid the "Now who was he?" reaction when seeing a given name for the first time in many pages.

DEDICATION

To Dr. David Campbell and Dr. Allen Gammon, two men never honored for their courage in speaking out at great personal sacrifice for the well-being of patients and the integrity of their university.

TABLE OF CONTENTS

PROLOGUE

SEPTEMBER 1983

"Genevieve, block that eye." The surgeon, gowned and gloved, pointed to the patient's left eye. Genevieve Switz hesitated, and as she later recalled, looked around for the operative permit. As the physician's assistant, she always checked the op permit one last time before an operation began. She had barely stepped into the room; everything was rush-rush. It was 6:00 PM, and this was the thirteenth operation of another long, hard day.

"Come on. Let's go." Genevieve heard the stress in his voice. She proceeded to block the eye without looking at the permit.

The patient lay sedated and oblivious while Genevieve pierced his left lower lid with the 26-gauge needle—a needle quite sharp, thin, and long—and maneuvered the tip to a position behind the eye. Five cubic centimeters of Xylocaine filled the space, paralyzing the muscles that move the eye and numbing the pain nerves.

The surgeon, H. Dwight Cavanagh—M.D., PhD, professor of ophthalmology and department chairman at Emory University School of Medicine in Atlanta—prepared to perform a corneal transplant with removal of cataract and insertion of lens implant.

First he sewed a ring to the sclera, the "white" of the eye, to prevent collapse later in the operation when the eye was open and vulnerable. Cavanagh had almost finished attaching the ring when

Dr. Philip Newman, the senior cornea fellow who was Cavanagh's first assistant, entered. Newman would remember Cavanagh's icy look and reprimand for the patient's poorly dilated pupil. In cataract surgery, the pupil should be dilated before the patient enters the room. Newman mumbled an apology and busied himself with the donor cornea. Newman turned the tissue upside down and picked up a circular cutting tool to punch out a dime-sized button from the center of the cornea.

Meanwhile, Cavanagh twirled a slightly smaller instrument through the center of the patient's own cornea until only a tiny barrier kept the circular blade from penetrating the eye. Using scissors to cut into the eye, he removed the smaller button, leaving the eye open and exposed. This is a critical moment. If the patient coughs or moves, the contents of the eye could spill out, leaving the eye forever blind. Speed counted now, while the cataract was removed and replaced.

Still grumbling about the insufficiently dilated pupil, Cavanagh demonstrated what must be done to the cataract when pupils are not dilated. Pushing the iris aside to gain room, the surgeon removed the cloudy lens and placed a plastic lens exactly where the old one had resided for seventy-four years. Coaxing the button of clear donor cornea into the slightly smaller ring of remaining host cornea, he swiftly placed a silk suture at 3:00, 6:00, 9:00, and 12:00. With the graft in place, the eye had a barrier—a clearer barrier—to the outside world. Everyone began breathing again. Another success, and with an operation not easily performed.

Dr. Cavanagh turned to Dr. Newman and instructed him to finish the case and left to dictate the operative reports. Newman must have appreciated Cavanagh's dictating his own notes, especially since Cavanagh required two reports for each operation, where other surgeons only required one. Most surgeons assigned this tedious work to assistants, so Dr. Newman was lucky.

It took Newman thirty minutes and twenty-four bites of the needle to run a suture smaller than a human hair, a suture that provided continuous closure to supplement the four silk sutures placed by Dr. Cavanagh. Then Newman sewed the patient's eyelids partially shut to protect the surface of the new graft.

Meanwhile, Cavanagh dictated two separate notes about the operation. He first described the intraocular portion of the surgery—the removal of the lens and placement of the corneal transplant. The second note detailed the extraocular portion of the surgery, the part where the lids were sewed partially shut. During the thirty minutes it took Newman to complete the surgery, Cavanagh also dictated the notes for his other twelve cases. All the cases had gone well. He was one of the busiest corneal surgeons in the nation and justly proud of it.

Dictation finished, Cavanagh had barely settled into the lounge when Philip Newman burst into the room. "We need to operate on the other eye as soon as we can," blurted Dr. Newman, then turned and fled. A few minutes later, the anesthesiologist came in. "Dwight, we have a problem, a big problem. You operated on the left eye, his good eye. You were supposed to do the right."

The next day, the patient woke up blind.

CHAPTER ONE

BEGINNINGS

1976

Dr. Dwight Cavanagh had top credentials and honors. He had earned not only a medical degree from Johns Hopkins, where only a tiny percent of applicants were admitted, but a PhD in biochemistry from Harvard, where he worked in the laboratory of Harvard's Nobel laureate George Wald. After his internship, he took a residency at the Wilmer Institute, the eye department of Johns Hopkins. After his residency, Cavanagh took a cornea fellowship, the final year of specialty training, at Harvard's Massachusetts Eye and Ear Infirmary. Another fellow at the time remembered that Cavanagh stood out for his brilliance and lucid discussions even at that early stage of his career. The faculty and attending staff led the world of ophthalmology, and few people could impress Harvard in this way.

Cavanagh came to Emory in the fall of 1976 as an assistant professor, eager to pursue his dream of success at a university medical center. He peered at the world through thick, wire-rimmed glasses. Thirty-six years old, tall, erect, white lab coat always buttoned and crisp, he commanded attention. With a rapid pigeon-toed gait, he would charge through the halls, residents and fellows trailing behind.

When he walked, his body tilted forward, head leading shoulders and hips. He always appeared to be in a hurry.

Articulate, charming, and sincere, he particularly impressed patients. He held their hands, looked intensely into their eyes, pattered on for a minute or so, all the while leading them toward the exit door since he knew other patients were waiting. They would leave in love.

I first met Cavanagh when I arrived on the Johns Hopkins campus in the summer of 1971. I was a first-year resident in ophthalmology at the Wilmer Institute of Johns Hopkins, twenty-six years old, a rookie; Cavanagh was a second-year resident, one of five who, along with the third-year residents and the chief resident, would teach us newcomers the ropes. He manifested his management talent to me early in that first year, when I was in the Wilmer emergency room at 2:00 in the morning wrestling with my first case of an attack of glaucoma. Cavanagh was my backup, so I called for advice. He heard my description, told me what to do, and he was definitely right. The treatment broke the attack, and all was well by morning rounds.

Two short years after his arrival at Emory and one year before the scheduled retirement of the current chairman, the university appointed Cavanagh chairman of the Department of Ophthalmology. Week after week Cavanagh mesmerized students and staff at teaching conferences with his brilliant synthesis of research and clinical data pertaining to particular patients' problems. When he spoke extemporaneously about the cases presented, he would often cite numerous journal references. He knew personal information about most of the researchers whose papers he quoted, and he always recited their credentials. Cavanagh was well acquainted with everyone on the cutting edge of eye research. Credentials mattered to Cavanagh.

I had come to Atlanta to practice in 1975, joining a group in downtown Atlanta. I attended these teaching conferences for years and was continually awed by Dwight's fund of knowledge, both clinical and scientific. Few could touch him when it came to case discussions.

Cavanagh had a wonderful vision for his department. He would build for himself one of the world's biggest practices in corneal-disease treatment. As chairman, he would lead his department to the top ranks of teaching and research institutions, rivaling Hopkins and the Ivy Leagues. He would build the new eye center promised to Emory faculty since the 1960s. He would raise the funds and ensure the eye center's mission to bring together patient care, surgery, research, and collegiality among young, outstanding, energetic doctors in one building. It would be world class.

But in the years that followed, it became apparent that Cavanagh's dreams did not end with the building of the eye center. He wanted research and academic renown as well. He would direct research fellows and PhDs, and together they would write papers that would be published in leading journals and read worldwide. His faculty would do the same in their subspecialties. Born in Atlanta's Piedmont Hospital, Cavanagh had returned to the city of his birth to a department and university ripe for growth and direction.

Our chairman at Johns Hopkins was a world power in ophthalmology. If the events of this book had not taken place, Cavanagh might have exceeded him. Starting with Emory's chairmanship, he might have progressed to the chairmanship at Harvard or head of the National Eye Institute.

He set to work. From 1978 to 1980, Cavanagh attracted specialists from academic centers across the United States and vastly increased the research funding and capability of the department. He began raising the $10 million ($22 million in 2008) necessary for construction of the new eye center while fending off opposition from other Emory faculty, who viewed the eye as a minor appendage of the body and not deserving of a building of its own. He oversaw many of the details for construction of the eye center. His own surgical practice expanded, and he took on responsibilities with national organizations.

One of the technicians marveled that within a few minutes of meeting someone, and after only a few questions, Dr. Cavanagh could tell that person what to do with the rest of his or her life and would be correct. He had great insight. He was one of the hardest-working people she had seen, paying close attention to detail. She said he noticed everything. Every Saturday, Cavanagh went to Grady Hospital, the downtown Atlanta hospital where the residents performed much of their work, to teach the doctors in training. He wanted to make good ophthalmologists of the doctors he admitted to his training program. He grew busier and busier, and his duties pulled him in many directions.

During these early years, Dwight Cavanagh grew close socially and professionally with two faculty members who came to Emory about the same time as he did—doctors David Campbell and Frank Bell. They and their wives got together on weekends, and Cavanagh dubbed them the "Three Musketeers."

David Campbell had a bright future. After Yale Medical School, Dr. Campbell had gone to Harvard for his eye residency, glaucoma training and, early on, a faculty appointment. The Campbells spent summers in Woods Hole on Cape Cod and were used to the cold northeastern winters. Six feet tall and blond-haired, the conservatively dressed Campbell impressed people as straitlaced, but in reality he was a man with a lively, if quiet, sense of humor.

Encouraged by Dwight Cavanagh even before he became chairman, David Campbell joined the Emory faculty in 1977. All Saints Episcopal Church attracted the Campbell family, and the kids were enrolled in good private schools. All the Campbells loved Atlanta, with its mild winters and long springs, and David had negotiated a month each summer for them to return to Woods Hole. Here at Emory, family settled, Dr. Campbell set out to meet his goals—to do valuable eye research, treat glaucoma patients and, most importantly, put down deep roots for his family. David Campbell never suspected that Dwight Cavanagh's dazzling energy and enthusiasm would irreparably damage his family's life, reputation, and career.

In David Campbell's first three years at Emory, he built a busy clinical practice but always gave time for teaching and research. He made weekly trips to Grady Hospital, the downtown public hospital staffed by Emory's faculty, residents, fellows, and medical students. He expanded the glaucoma clinic at Grady, affording more specialized care to Atlanta's poorest citizens as well as more focused teaching for the residents.

At Emory, Campbell continued the research he began at Harvard, studying two types of glaucoma, pigmentary glaucoma and a syndrome dubbed ICE (iridocorneal endothelial syndrome). In 1979 a prominent national organization, Research to Prevent Blindness, named Campbell the Robert McCormick Scholar, a coveted award recognizing him as an outstanding young researcher. Even more significant, the National Eye Institute awarded him a grant in September 1979 to study pigmentary glaucoma. This grant named Campbell the principal investigator and extended funding over six years, allowing him to expand his lab and hire other scientists.

David Campbell's activities didn't stop with research and teaching. Residents and fellows sought his advice. They trusted him. His honesty and conservatism shone through every encounter. A few described him as puritanical, but only a few. And all members of the department regarded him as their conscience. Consequently, residents sought his counsel between patients, in the halls, and after hours. Where could they go into practice? Which was better, academics or private practice? What should they do with their lives?

After two years of Dr. Cavanagh's hard work, cracks in the foundation of his well-constructed department began to appear. Cavanagh grew frantically busy, so busy that his activities generated concern not only from colleagues within his department but also from the highest levels of Emory's administration.

As 1980 began, the tenor of David Campbell's discussions with the young doctors shifted and reflected these cracks. Activities on campus dominated the conversations, especially the patterns of Dwight Cavanagh's practice. They insisted on talking with Campbell behind closed doors. The discussions—hesitant and with lowered voices—centered on Campbell's chairman, friend, and fellow musketeer, Dwight Cavanagh.

* * *

OCTOBER 1980

Dr. James Glenn came to Emory as dean of the medical school from Duke University. Soon after Dean Glenn arrived at Emory in early 1980, he began to hear complaints about Dwight Cavanagh. Years later, in preparation for his testimony in one of the lawsuits precipitated by the events of this book, he told a lawyer, *I began receiving numerous phone calls from patients on a regular basis, some of whom had driven in from out of town for appointments with Cavanagh and been required to wait as long as five or six hours past the time of their scheduled appointment. And when they finally got in, Cavanagh spent all of two or three minutes with them because he still had a long line of other patients waiting outside the door. Cavanagh was not spending enough time with the patients to perform any kind of meaningful examination or establish a proper rapport with the patients.... On several occasions, I was performing surgery myself in one of the operating rooms close to the operating rooms Cavanagh was using, and I observed that this surgery schedule listed more major surgeries than anyone could properly perform in one day...*

Glenn continued his story to the lawyer, relating the details of a meeting in his office with Cavanagh in late 1980. *I told him it was clearly unfair to the patients to see that many in one day.... I told him no doctor could hope to complete that many surgeries in a day without taking a substantial risk of a mistake.... I told him that as dean of the medical school, I was instructing him to reduce the volume of his practice to a level commensurate with his ability to render good-quality patient care.*

After ordering Cavanagh to change, Glenn headed home in the dark, hoping his direct order would produce results. A dean's direct orders should produce results, but though he ran the medical school and faculty, Glenn did not have full authority on campus. It was complicated. The several hundred Emory University doctors, when seeing patients, did not do so as university employees, as it is in many medical schools. These doctors actually practiced in the Emory Clinic, a group practice independent of the medical school and Dean Glenn. The clinic was run by Dr. Charles Hatcher, an outstanding heart surgeon. Most of the Emory doctors' incomes flowed through the clinic. Money generates power, and Glenn had not yet fully realized the extent of Dr. Hatcher's influence and the consequent limitations imposed on Glenn's own power and his ability to make changes in the activity of his faculty.

* * *

JANUARY *1981*

Dr. David Campbell remembers Dwight Cavanagh dropping down to the third floor of the clinic, the location of director Charles Hatcher's office, on a regular basis. Each had something to teach the other, and they enjoyed each other's company. Hatcher knew about department and practice finances; Cavanagh knew about the funds to be gained from research grants.

Dr. Charles Hatcher, born in 1930, grew up in Attapulgus, a town in southwest Georgia near the Florida line. After a residency in heart surgery at Johns Hopkins, he turned down a position there to come to his first choice, Emory. He pioneered heart surgery at Emory and in the state of Georgia, performing a number of firsts—the first successful blue-baby surgery, the first heart-valve replacements, and the first coronary bypass, among others. His obvious administrative talents led to his election as head of the Emory Clinic in 1976. Over the five years of his directorship, Hatcher had gradually reduced his clinical load of heart surgeries in order to make room for his increasing administrative responsibilities. Yet he kept his administrative office on the third floor, the cardiovascular floor, the source of his income. He made financial decisions for his cardiovascular partners and the clinic. No one doubted that Hatcher, a born leader, ran things. Strong and charming, he had a commanding personality. A member of Atlanta's social elite, he had gained membership in the leading social club and the downtown Rotary Club, where Atlanta's business leaders met weekly.

CHAPTER TWO

PROBLEMS: 1982

FEBRUARY 1982

In 1982 most of the Emory Clinic doctors were crammed into one building, the Scarborough building, with ophthalmology and four other specialties sharing the fifth floor. Patients coming to the eye department turned to the right off the elevator and headed down the hallway to check in. Dwight Cavanagh, in practice now for six years, had so many patients on Tuesdays and Wednesdays that the waiting rooms overflowed. The space could not accommodate a hundred or so patients plus family members spending the day as they waited their turns. Thirty or more patients filled extra chairs lining the hall, wherever they could fit amongst patients in wheelchairs or standing or using walkers. White-coated faculty, residents, fellows, and technicians threaded their way through this obstacle course.

Across from Cavanagh's office, down the hall jutting off to Psychiatry, sat three bins of charts for the patients of the day. First an assistant took the relevant history from the patient, reviewed the tests, did an examination, and placed the chart in a pile near Cavanagh's secretary. She decided who would be seen next and would place that patient near Cavanagh's door.

Into this scene, and not for the first time, came two patients: Gladys Wilson and her mother. Her 1986 deposition revealed the following. Wilson, born in Alton Park, Tennessee, on April 13, 1911, had lived in Decatur, Georgia, for twenty-four years. She had taken early retirement from Delta Airlines in 1962. Wilson's mother, now in her nineties and under Wilson's care, had worked on the eye floor at Emory years before and had even had several eye operations there. By 1982 Gladys Wilson found it difficult to care for her mother. She no longer trusted herself driving. She began to miss street signs, occasionally getting lost in her own town, and couldn't tell whether a traffic signal was green or red. Her husband had a part-time job that he didn't want to give up in order to drive Gladys around and aid in caring for her mother.

Wilson and her mother were both Dr. Cavanagh's patients and were accustomed to the three-to-four-hour wait. Wilson knew the routine: no trips to the bathroom after the secretary had the charts. If she called while they were in there, it would be another two hours.

When at last their turn came, Cavanagh, charts in hand, helped them down the hall to his office, charming them with small talk. Mother in the exam chair, light from the scope on each eye; out of the chair, time for the daughter. One minute for the mother, one minute for Gladys, and then time to discuss the treatment plan.

Gladys Wilson had referred herself to Dwight Cavanagh for problems with cataracts. Cataract surgery in the 1980s had improved significantly over the previous ten years. A cataract is a clouding of the normally clear lens that occupies the front third of the eye. When haziness occurs, the term *cataract* applies. Heretofore, cataract surgery consisted of removing the entire cloudy lens, forcing the patient to wear thick glasses or uncomfortable contact lenses. Surgeons could now implant an artificial lens. Intraocular lens (IOL) implantation rapidly became the gold standard for cataract surgery.

But Dr. Cavanagh told Wilson that, in addition to a cataract, she had a disease of her cornea. The cornea is the thin, transparent tissue that covers the front of the eye, analogous to the crystal of a watch.

It acts as a lens and begins the process of focusing light on the back of the eye. The cornea is about as thin as a credit card and slightly bigger than a nickel.

Cavanagh's diagnosis surprised Wilson. Her previous ophthalmologist had never mentioned corneal problems, only the cataracts, but Cavanagh was the expert, and she accepted his opinion.

Cavanagh then gave Wilson's mother to the technician for instructions and prescriptions. He turned to Wilson and told her she needed a "triple" (a corneal transplant, cataract extraction, and lens implantation). Wilson knew that Cavanagh had done this same operation on her mother's eyes. She knew that, despite Cavanagh's assurance that the operation was successful, her mother had remained blind. But unlike Wilson, her mother also had glaucoma. So, notwithstanding the inevitable doubts that arise when we are faced with surgery that has not gone well for someone we know, Wilson agreed and scheduled the surgery. She did request that she have no further contact with Dr. Cavanagh's fellow at the time, Dr. Leaper (not his real name). She felt he had treated her rudely and wanted no more of him. Gladys Wilson wanted to be treated only by Dr. Cavanagh himself.

* * *

According to his tech, Dr. Cavanagh often joked as he entered the operating room, "These hands have been touched by God." But as Cavanagh proceeded through Gladys Wilson's operation, he must have muttered the words his technicians had come to dread, the words Cavanagh would always and only say when he had problems in surgery: "Perfect, perfect."

As soon as the tech heard the sarcastic "Perfect, perfect," he knew the eye was in trouble, and indeed it was. The lens sac, or capsule—a membrane that surgeons strive to keep intact—had ruptured. Worse, swelling of the tissues from the back of the eye threatened to extrude and ruin the eye completely.

With a crisis like this, the words would flow from the surgeon: "Come on, where's the button? Get that blood pressure down. That's where this fluid is coming from. Hold this here. Suture, suture. Perfect, perfect. Hurry, hurry, and give me another suture."

With sticky, vitreous gel from behind the lens sac all over the place, Cavanagh placed as many sutures as he could. He was unable to put in a lens implant but did transplant her cornea, averting the disaster of a lost eye. Without an intraocular lens, she would be able to see, but only if she could tolerate a contact lens.

The operation brought only misery to Wilson. In the days after her operation, her eye flashed and flickered, and she never saw well. Her eye hurt most of the day, every day. It also drained fluid and felt like something was in it. She was puzzled. Cavanagh had told her that her eye was too small for a lens implant and that she would eventually need a contact lens. He emphasized that "the eye is fine," so Wilson wasn't too concerned. Then he left town, leaving her in the care of his cornea fellow, whom she did not like and whom she had requested not be involved in her care.

Now home after a week in the hospital, she had her husband Arthur call Cavanagh's office every day, only to learn that the cornea fellow was still taking calls for his chief. She would have none of that.

After three weeks, Gladys Wilson called the secretary. She had to see somebody, she said, anybody but that cornea fellow. Her eye had developed a shade that blocked part of her vision. The next day she saw Dr. Doyle Stulting, another cornea fellow. He found trouble.

Dr. Henry Kaplan, the senior retina specialist, confirmed Stulting's diagnosis of retinal detachment. The retina is the thin tissue that lines the back of the eye. Light rays bent by the cornea and lens are focused on the retina, which sends nerve impulses that the brain translates into vision. When fluid accumulates behind the retina, it balloons forward and detaches. Untreated, a detached retina causes blindness. Surgery is the only treatment.

Kaplan's words shocked Wilson. Emergency surgery on an eye that Dr. Cavanagh said was "fine," retinal detachment related to complications at the first surgery, complications never disclosed to her. Her worst nightmare, all in a rush.

Dr. Hank Kaplan had arrived on campus in 1978, a Cavanagh recruit from the University of Wisconsin with great research potential. Kaplan had a PhD in immunology in addition to a retinal fellowship. He could not only develop a retinal practice but also get government money for retinal research. Kaplan produced results in both his clinical practice and research.

Gladys Wilson had her first retinal-detachment operation in March, a month after Cavanagh had operated. Throughout the procedure, Kaplan worked hard, both hands and both feet busy. One hand controlled the main instrument, a long, thin pipe that cut and extracted bands of scar tissue. The other hand controlled the light pipe that illuminated the inside of the eye. The left foot worked the pedal of the operating microscope while the right regulated the pace of the cutting.

Looking through the microscope for almost transparent bands of scarring, Kaplan noted, as detailed in his operative report, a lot of vitreous on the back of the graft. When the lens sac ruptures in surgery, the vitreous gel needs to be removed or it will stick to the structures of the eye, contract, and pull the retina loose, detaching it. The amount of vitreous stuck to Wilson's graft indicated an inadequate cleanup at the first surgery.

Typically when a surgeon cleans up a colleague's mess, it's not easy. When the colleague has not mentioned complications to the patient or prepared the patient for problems, and the surgeon has to endure the shocked anger of the patient as well as undo the damage, it's even harder. Fortunately for Gladys Wilson, she was unconscious and blessedly unaware of the future of her eye.

* * *

MARCH 1982

Dean Jim Glenn paced the length of Dr. Charles Hatcher's office and back. After two frustrating years and three formal meetings with Dr. Cavanagh, Glenn had seen no change in Cavanagh's office or surgical schedule. Glenn took the problem to Hatcher. Glenn had recently heard of another aberration in Cavanagh's practice, that of using residents in corneal-transplant surgery but submitting bills as if another type of doctor, a fellow, had assisted.

A fellow is a doctor in the last phase of medical training. You become a fellow after four years of medical school, one year of internship, and three years of residency. Instead of going into practice as a general ophthalmologist, a fellow serves one or two more years to become a subspecialist in one of several areas—glaucoma, cornea, retina, pediatrics, or plastic surgery, to name a few. Because fellows have completed residency training, Medicare and other insurance companies allow training programs to bill for their services in certain situations. Residents, on the other hand, are doctors still in training and not yet fully fledged ophthalmologists. The federal government pays universities to train residents, so Medicare does not allow a program to bill for them. When a training program has both residents and fellows, Medicare assumes that residents are available to help in surgery and thus doesn't allow separate billing for fellows. Cavanagh was billing Medicare and insurance companies for fellows' services when only residents were in the room. A fellow could bill $600 ($1300 in 2008) for assisting on a triple, a significant amount for a training program always looking for dollars.

Glenn had seen the following letter of justification that Cavanagh sent to the insurance companies when they challenged Cavanagh's practice of billing for fellows as assistants in some of Cavanagh's operations.

Dear Sir:

Emory University School of Medicine, Department of Ophthalmology, is the leading referral center for corneal transplantation work in the United States.... It should be clearly understood that corneal transplantation operation is a highly complex technical operative procedure which requires...

Residents have never been allowed to assist at this surgery at Emory University School of Medicine, Department of Ophthalmology; nor are they taught this procedure as an undergraduate in eye surgery training....

To entrust this to the level of a beginner would not only not be in the patient's best interest but in my opinion would constitute malpractice...

From this information, it should be rapidly and easily seen that an assistant's fee to a senior physician is not only justified in this case but depriving the patient of such skilled assistance could be construed as acting against their best interest directly.

With warmest personal wishes and thanks for your consideration...

> *H. Dwight Cavanagh, M.D., Ph.D.*
> *Professor and Chairman*
> *Department of Ophthalmology*

In the later trial preparation, Glenn told the attorney: "At some point, it came to my attention that Cavanagh was billing for assistant surgeons used in cornea transplants. I told him I didn't know how he could justify doing that, that no other teaching hospital I'd ever been affiliated with had done that, and that it was clearly illegal to bill for assistant surgeons in a teaching hospital if a qualified person on the staff of the hospital, such as a resident or intern, was available to provide such services."

When the attorney asked Glenn's opinion of the above letter, he replied, "This is preposterous. Most of the cornea surgeons I know in private practice routinely perform cornea transplants without any assistant surgeon. It is basically a one-man operation."

Glenn then told the attorney Hatcher's response to Glenn's concerns about Cavanagh, "I know all of that, but I can control him." A frustrated Dean Glenn left, determined to pursue the matter in other ways.

* * *

The resident assigned to ocular pathology was bent over his microscope. He had a question for Dr. John Wright, the faculty member who doubled as a pediatric ophthalmologist and ocular pathologist. The slide under the microscope had a tissue reading from Gladys Wilson's cornea.

Dr. Cavanagh's diagnosis of Gladys Wilson's disease was Fuchs' dystrophy, but the resident could not see the signs of this disease as he looked at the tissue.

Pathologists at all hospitals examine tissue removed at surgery and make a diagnosis, a pathological diagnosis. They compare their diagnosis to the clinical diagnosis sent by the surgeon submitting the tissue sample. Mismatches between the diagnoses of the pathologist and the surgeon are rare. When they occur, the surgeon has some explaining to do. In fact, in some departments such as general surgery, entire monthly conferences center on these unusual occurrences. No such monthly conferences were held in the eye department.

Dr. Wright had been on campus for seven months. By now he was not surprised at the resident's problem, but Wright would look himself to be sure. The findings of this disease can be subtle or alternately obvious on different slices of the patient's tissue. But in the case of Gladys Wilson, both the resident and Dr. Wright confirmed that her cornea was healthy. Fuchs' dystrophy is easy to spot in patients with significant vision loss. It's easy to see in the office, and it's easy to see in the pathology lab. When a patient with a healthy cornea is subjected to surgery unnecessarily, the pathologist can tell by the lack of significant findings under the microscope.

Dr. John Wright later testified that he had seen a number of totally normal corneal specimens from Cavanagh's surgery in his seven months. Dr. Cavanagh had diagnosed a disease and operated, but Wright had found no sign of any abnormality. So he had a dilemma and a big responsibility. He had accurately reported his findings on each patient, including, as revealed in her later lawsuit, placing a report in Wilson's chart noting the absence of Fuchs' dystrophy. He hoped that a report of a normal cornea would elicit concern from Dr. Cavanagh. No query came.

John Wright crossed the street looking for the head of general pathology. He found him amidst the usual chaos—phones ringing from surgeons asking where their frozen section reading was, techs cutting tissue, organs being delivered fresh from surgery in large metal pans.

As soon as the department chairman looked up, John Wright unloaded his burden. Wright had a problem, needed help. Corneal transplants with no disease, cases with minimal disease, what was Wright to do when they came from the chairman, the boss? Dr. Cavanagh doesn't comment on the reports.

He testified that the normal tissue came from only one of the three corneal surgeons, Dwight Cavanagh. Dr. Wright told him there were too many to count if you include the minimal cases, five to ten of totally normal corneas. No, talking to him wouldn't help. So Wright wanted advice on what to do.

The chief said to put a label on the normal ones, Code 3, and send them over to him. Code 3 means the pathology doesn't match the surgeon's diagnosis. A special committee of pathologists, the Tissue Committee, reviewed all such cases from throughout the hospital and would summon the surgeon for an explanation. A relieved

Wright discharged his responsibility by sending over his Code 3 cases. In his experience, Cavanagh would not question him about the path reports on the chart, but he trusted the system to rectify his growing problem.

* * *

James T. Laney, PhD, president of Emory University, must have sighed when he saw Dean Jim Glenn on his schedule. Jim Glenn, not again, always complaining, never happy. Dr. Laney, a graduate of Yale Divinity School and an ordained Methodist minister, had studied and written on ethics and the moral life. *Harvard Magazine* had published his article "The Education of the Heart," and it was widely quoted. He struck you as the perfect university president. Solid in body, with a reassuring, pastoral voice, he exuded calmness, solemnity, and the ability to solve the gravest of problems.

Laney spent most of his time developing the nonmedical areas of the university, thinking perhaps that the medical center was already dominant. But he did monitor health affairs. Dean Glenn told his attorney that he knew that one of the highlights of President Laney's week was the trip from campus to downtown Atlanta with Charles Hatcher and Garland Herndon, the vice president for health affairs, to the Atlanta Rotary Club. There they mixed with Atlanta's business leaders, some of whom, including my uncle, were on Emory's board. On the return trip, the three would decide issues and weekly jobs for their subordinates, including Jim Glenn. Dr. Herndon was Dean Glenn's superior, yet, despite the protocols of hierarchy, sometimes Glenn would insist on talking to the president.

If Laney hoped he would get good news, he was wrong. Jim Glenn had come to warn Laney about Dwight Cavanagh. Glenn's attempts at solving the matter lower in the chain of command with Charles Hatcher had failed; he had a duty to talk to the ultimate boss. Glenn recalls that he laid out the familiar story—patient volume too large, too many complaints, headed for trouble, "that unless something could be done about him, patients would be injured and the reputation of the medical school would be damaged."

Then Dean Glenn, unaware of the close friendship between Laney and Hatcher, says he warned Laney about Hatcher, whom Glenn had come to distrust. Dean Glenn told President Laney that Dr. Hatcher was a liability to the university, in large part because Hatcher had failed to rein in Dwight Cavanagh. Laney, Glenn recalls, said he would get back to him.

Dean Glenn told his lawyer he got the word from his boss, the vice president, a few weeks later: "Get off Cavanagh's back... Cavanagh was too valuable and was bringing in too much money and they didn't want to interfere with him."

* * *

Dwight Cavanagh beamed as he approached his patient's bedside. Cavanagh had operated on Mattie Brown, giving her a new cornea and a lens implant. The diagnoses: Fuchs' dystrophy and cataract. He was optimistic on this visit and all future ones. Brown recalled the litany in a 1987 deposition: "You're going to get a good eye, Mattie. Hang in there." Then off he ran. She said she never saw him walk.

Mattie Sue Brown, almost seventy-five years old, had come from Calhoun, Georgia, a small town sixty miles north of Atlanta. She liked to garden and do handwork. Her local doctor had diagnosed cataracts and changed her glasses until new ones no longer helped. She had four land lots to care for and plant flowers in, and she couldn't see to garden anymore. She could not do her beloved handwork. Sunlight blinded her, and driving was more and more a problem. A lively, talkative lady, Mattie Brown wanted her independence. She needed help.

When Mattie Sue Brown said that sunlight "kindly blinds you," she referred to glare problems common to some cataracts. As the normally clear human lens becomes opaque and cataractous, patients experience vision difficulties in different ways. Less light reaches the back of the eye, so everything appears dimmer. "Turn up the lights" is a common request even when, to unaffected family members, room lights seem too bright already. The ability to discern contrast between an object and its background diminishes, making small bumps in a walkway invisible. Walking becomes more uncertain; golf balls disappear. Wrinkles disappear in the mirror, as do crumbs on the floor or dust on the furniture. When some patients finally get a clear view of their wrinkles for the first time in years, they jokingly wish for their cataracts back.

Some cataracts scatter light, producing glare. In this case, driving with the sun behind you is easy. But driving into the sun nearly blinds you. Headlights at night flare, making night driving particularly difficult.

Mattie Brown knew that the Calhoun Lions Club sold brooms and mops, donating the proceeds to Emory's eye bank. After a good experience with an Emory internist, she solicited his recommendation for an Emory ophthalmologist and, from the two names given her, chose Dwight Cavanagh. She had seen many eye doctors in her past, but Cavanagh particularly impressed her. She wanted the best for her eyes and willingly trekked back and forth between home and Emory. On every visit after the surgery, even though she was seeing poorly, Cavanagh would tell her she had a good eye and pat her shoulder as they walked to the side door. In her 1987 deposition, Brown's daughter Lois recalled the stock phrase Cavanagh would say to the family: "Take her home and keep her happy."

After looking at Mattie Brown's corneal button, seeing no sign of Fuchs' dystrophy and duly noting it in the chart, Dr. John Wright must have wondered how many more normal corneas he was going to see. He forwarded yet another Code 3 case to the General Pathology Department's tissue committee and wondered when he would get feedback from his previous cases.

* * *

Meanwhile, the eye department continued to grow. Dr. Doyle Stulting, who had diagnosed Gladys Wilson's retinal detachment when he was a fellow, joined the faculty, in part to relieve Dr. Cavanagh of some of his patient load.

The Atlanta community of ophthalmologists viewed Emory's growth with mixed feelings. We knew that an outstanding academic program helped the city and indeed the state. Yet new faculty members meant more competition for patients. As fellowships across the country pumped out graduates, more and more subspecialists came to Atlanta, some in individual practices, some to my group, Eye Consultants of Atlanta, at Piedmont Hospital. Our group collaborated with Emory on clinical studies while competing for referrals from individual general ophthalmologists. We spent considerable time discussing the threat Emory posed to us. Yet, while group-to-group interactions were occasionally strained, most of us remained friends on a personal level. My friendship with David Campbell grew; I attended most of the eye department's social occasions, including parties at Dwight Cavanagh's home. We had been friends at Johns Hopkins, and our wives regarded each other warmly. He and I rarely saw each other one-on-one, but we regarded our common Hopkins experience as a bond. The Cavanaghs lived distant from the Emory campus in the beautiful and exclusive Buckhead area, nearer Atlanta's leading private schools.

* * *

JULY 1982

Gladys Wilson, now dismissed by Dr. Kaplan, was back in Cavanagh's office. Her later deposition revealed the details. Wilson's eye was blind. Three retina operations had failed. Worse, the eye still hurt. Her husband had quit his part-time job to drive Gladys and her mother around and care for them. Now they had only retirement income to make ends meet.

Gladys recounted his words in her deposition: "Well, you know God did this to you. Your family must have a curse on it." He switched to the right eye, declaring that it had the same diseases as the left, cataract and Fuchs', and would soon need a triple.

Around this time, a surprising incident caught everyone's attention. The fire marshal was on the eye floor of the clinic. He had come at the order of the DeKalb county commissioner, Manuel Maloof. The husband of Cavanagh's main technologist, Mary Gemmill, tired of her complaints about the overcrowding, stress, and twelve-hour days, had tipped Maloof off about the crowding of the hallways.

Cavanagh came out of his office to find the DeKalb County fire marshal demanding to speak with him. One day earlier, the marshal's deputy had instructed Cavanagh to clear the hall of the extra chairs. Had a fire erupted, no one could have made it out through the maze and obstruction posed by the clutter. Cavanagh had shaken hands with the deputy, ignored his orders, and Ollie, Gemmill's husband, had called the county commissioner again.

This time the message was emphatic: "Clear the chairs within the hour or I will shut you down." The chairs disappeared, never to jam the halls again. Mary Gemmill's husband had hoped to reduce the volume of patients in Cavanagh's practice by denying them close places to sit, but he hoped in vain. The patients kept coming and had to pack themselves into even more crowded waiting rooms.

The incident amazed the entire faculty. The typical visit from the fire department was invisible, and a doctor's clinic day had never been threatened with cancellation before.

* * *

The fire-marshal story added to David Campbell's worry about Dwight Cavanagh's practice. Campbell was busy, very busy. He had built such a large practice that a second faculty member in glaucoma, Dr. Robert Allen, had just arrived. Yet the secretive visits from worried residents and fellows had continued, even escalating since

1980. The growing concern about Cavanagh remained Campbell's only source of discontent at Emory. Campbell was worried about Cavanagh himself, since he knew about a gastric ulcer that Cavanagh had developed, and about the patients. Dr. Campbell felt that he should try to work with Dr. Cavanagh personally and privately, so he made an appointment for a meeting.

David Campbell didn't know it, but he was not alone in hearing about problems in the department. Dr. George Waring also had become aware. Waring, the first cornea subspecialist recruited by Cavanagh, had joined the Emory eye department in 1979. A rising star himself in national ophthalmology, he had moved from Sacramento, despite warnings from mutual colleagues. The doctors in American cornea circles who knew both Cavanagh and Waring had predicted that the two would never last in the same department. Tall, adventurous, and athletic, Waring wore glasses almost as thick as Cavanagh's. He had settled into an office on the other side of the elevator from Cavanagh, but "settled" did not define Waring, with his numerous projects and frequent travels. When he was in residence, he usually had a phone glued to his ear.

Residents and fellows repeatedly complained to Dr. Waring that Dr. Cavanagh operated on eyes that seemed to have only mild signs of disease. They noticed other senior corneal physicians rejecting surgery on such eyes, feeling they would not need surgery for many years, if ever. So many comments came that Waring had concocted a stock answer. In a 1984 letter to Cavanagh, Waring revealed the words he used: *One of the advantages of being at Emory is that we have a diverse faculty with different approaches to ophthalmic problems; this is part of the richness of the department.* That's what he said, and that was it. Then he would change the subject. George Waring didn't convey his concern to Dwight Cavanagh, but he was paying attention.

* * *

AUGUST 1982

David Campbell found Cavanagh cleaning off the top of his expansive, six-foot-wide desk before leaving for his summer vacation. Visitors in Cavanagh's office sat either in a chair to the side, with no direct view of Cavanagh, or on a low sofa directly facing him. Photographs of Cavanagh with chairmen from other eye departments and bookshelves lined the walls.

The Cavanagh family spent August on the coast of South Carolina in their beach condominium on Hilton Head Island, and Campbell wanted to reach him before he left. The two had worked closely the last five years, and Campbell was sure he could sway his friend and chief.

Campbell later testified that he told Cavanagh that Cavanagh was far too busy and needed to slow down, needed to give something up. Cavanagh needed to pass patients to his cornea colleagues, to lighten his load, to get his ulcer healed.

But Cavanagh said he couldn't cut back. He could handle it. At Hopkins they learned to work hard. If he kept going, this would be a great department. The department would get a good ranking. Campbell needed to support him.

Cavanagh moved quickly on to fund-raising and then questions about Campbell's research, touching on anything and everything except the very subject Campbell wanted to pursue.

He went on and on, until he finally wished Campbell a great time on Cape Cod. Campbell watched Cavanagh head for his month off and wondered how long this could continue.

CHAPTER THREE

COMING CRISIS

OCTOBER 1982

Dr. Allen Gammon hated Cavanagh's clinic days. Every Tuesday and Wednesday he heard the patients complaining as they passed his office and disappeared into Cavanagh's, just next door.

Gammon had joined the Ophthalmology Department in April 1980. He was a pediatric ophthalmologist, trained in both pediatrics and ophthalmology after graduating from the University of Kansas medical school. All pediatric ophthalmologists train an extra year after their eye residency; Gammon had gone the extra years of a pediatric residency before his eye training. He had arranged that his pediatric fellowship would involve training in Washington, D.C., New York City, and London, assuring exposure to the top names in the field. He had passed the board examinations in both disciplines. Now well into his thirties, he had begun to show a few gray hairs amidst the black ones. He was intense and to the point. He gave no quarter in a dispute and would not rest until he had won. Call him the bulldog.

In a later Emory Ethics Committee investigation, Gammon recalled the problems he encountered early on. The cornea fellows would often ask Gammon to examine Cavanagh's pediatric patients so the young patients and families wouldn't have to wait the typical four to six hours. To Gammon's dismay, Cavanagh would keep the eyes of infants patched for weeks and weeks, robbing the brain and the eye of the opportunity to interact so that vision could develop. Gammon wondered why you would operate at all if you patched the eyes this long. Finally, he could take it no longer.

Gammon later testified that he made an appointment with Dwight Cavanagh. He told Dr. Cavanagh of the multiple complaints heard on each clinic day, how Gammon lightened the load by seeing some of Cavanagh's babies. Cavanagh needed to slow down.

Cavanagh told him that's how he developed a busy practice—he saw all comers. If he started turning patients away, he would start to lose it. They could wait.

Gammon kept at it. Waiting was just part of the problem. Keeping the babies patched so long kept them from developing vision. Cavanagh's staff was too stressed, no lunch, no break, and sometimes no dinner.

Cavanagh told him that he wanted support from Gammon, not criticism. Cavanagh was working hard and would continue to do so, and Gammon was to find a way to help.

Frustrated, Gammon knew he would keep seeing the babies, not for the chief but for the babies' sakes. He would find a way to fix the other problems, too. It might just take a while.

* * *

MARCH 1983

President Jim Laney gave Dean James Glenn the news personally. Dr. Garland Herndon was too ill to continue as vice president of Health Affairs; Laney had no choice but to accept Herndon's resignation and relieve him of his duty. Laney had appointed two people as co–vice presidents—John Palms, the current vice president of the university, and Dr. Charles Hatcher.

Since Dr. Hatcher was more active in health affairs, Hatcher would become his boss. Dean Glenn had no intention of reporting to Dr. Hatcher or becoming subordinate to him in any way. He decided to resign. In his words, "You can quote me on this, money mattered more than anything in those days at Emory; more than quality, ethics, and honesty."

Glenn began looking for another job. A few months later, he became president of Mt. Sinai Medical Center at Mt. Sinai Hospital in New York City.

* * *

Dr. Alan Kozarsky had a problem. He had been a cornea fellow since July 1982, first working with Dr. George Waring and later with Dr. Cavanagh. Dr. Kozarsky saw that Dwight Cavanagh was altering patient records, so he took his concerns to George Waring. Dr. Kozarsky had observed that Cavanagh crossed out eye-pressure readings recorded on the chart by Dr. Kozarsky. Dr. Cavanagh wrote in lower numbers. High numbers mean glaucoma. A change to lower numbers makes it appear that glaucoma, a blinding disease, never existed. Kozarsky was fully trained. He and the experienced technicians knew how to measure pressure accurately. In some patients, Cavanagh wrote "FT normal." "FT" meant "finger tension," indicating that Cavanagh didn't use an instrument but would quickly touch the eye with his finger to estimate its degree of firmness, a method of pressure measurement that had been abandoned in ophthalmology decades earlier.

A second chart alteration involved vision measurement. Dr. Kozarsky worked with the patient to obtain a measurement of the vision, a difficult task with some of these patients. Cavanagh would strike through the vision recorded and substitute his own. Kozarsky noted that, if the patient was potentially facing surgery, Cavanagh would substitute a worse vision, thus making the patient appear more in need of surgery. If the patient had already had surgery,

Cavanagh's substitution would indicate better vision, thus making his surgical result look better on paper. Dr. David Campbell later testified that Alan Kozarsky told him there were between 500 and 1000 such chart alterations.

In medical practice, the chart reigns. Many people enter data on charts, especially on hospital charts. Everyone assumes honesty holds and that the chart notes are accurate. From early in training, junior doctors hear, "Is the chart right? Is the chart right?" The question means, does the hospital chart accurately reflect all the lab values, the original condition of the patient, the progress of the patient, and the final disposition? Or does the office chart accurately reflect the history, vision, pressure, other measurements, and the doctor's thoughts on the patient's condition? Documentation is everything. If you didn't record it, you didn't do it.

Ideally chart entries are never changed. In the real world, people occasionally write the wrong thing and need to make alterations. The correct way to make a change is to line through the incorrect entry in a manner that allows a reader to see what had been written originally, albeit incorrectly. Then you initial and date your entry so a reader knows who made the change.

A good way to ruin a malpractice defense is to change the chart, to try to hide the truth. Opposing attorneys chew up the hapless person who makes these changes, and juries reward plaintiffs accordingly. Every malpractice seminar stresses the correct way to change a chart. If you change the chart in desperation, get out your wallet and settle the case.

When lawsuits occur, everyone scrutinizes the chart and makes decisions more on chart findings than on plaintiffs' complaints or defendants' explanations. Few doctors cheat, but those who do learn very early to keep good charts.

As a result of their meeting, Waring's awareness was building. Kozarsky kept watching.

* * *

MAY 1983

His creased brown fedora planted to his balding head, Sargus Houston shuffled down the long hall of Emory's fifth floor and sat in Mary Gemmill's exam chair. He shuffled because his seventy-four-year-old knees didn't work too well, not because he couldn't see. He had one good eye and one bad eye but got through his days pretty well. He was here to see the big doctor.

Mary Gemmill was Cavanagh's number-one technologist, responsible for working up Cavanagh's new patients. Rushed and harried as usual, she wrote in the chart, "Can't see out of OD very well, has had poor V OD for two years." This meant the right eye—Oculus Dexter (OD)—had poor vision (V) for two years. His ophthalmologist in Macon, Georgia, Dr. J.O. Martin, had referred Houston to Cavanagh.

Sargus Houston had lived a simple life. Born in middle Georgia to a poor African-American family, he had worked either construction or farming after leaving the army in the late 1940s. His army duties took him to Cherbourg, France, where he served in the 711 Medical Unit handling dead bodies. He hadn't known it, but this unit was known as the "Emory Unit." He did remember that most of the doctors were from Georgia.

He spent eleven years working construction in Ohio, where he married and fathered a daughter. Sargus Houston left Ohio alone, without divorcing his wife, and returned to Georgia. In the late 1960s, his mind "got bad," and he had several short admissions to Georgia's public mental hospital in Milledgeville. These problems cleared, but he never worked again, subsisting on disability payments and living with one sister or another in Macon. His nephew, Dophus Davidson, had driven him the ninety miles from Macon to a niece's house, and he had spent a week with her awaiting his visit with Cavanagh.

Why did he come if he could see pretty well? He came because his doctor told him to. When you were old, poor, and African-American in middle Georgia in the 1980s, you grew up in a culture that discouraged questioning your doctor.

Gemmill further noted that Houston's vision was 20/300 in the right eye and 20/25 in the left eye. Roughly speaking, visual acuity of 20/300 means that his right eye could see at twenty feet what a normal eye could see at 300 feet. Vision at this level constitutes legal blindness. 20/25, the vision of the left eye, is essentially normal.

Hat in hand, he moved with Cavanagh from the hall to the private office.

The patter began. Sargus was having trouble with that right eye. Dr. Martin had said it may need some fixing up. Houston readily acknowledged that the right eye had poor vision.

Cavanagh noted that he had "lattice dystrophy 8+ OD, ½+ OS, cat OD." Lattice dystrophy is one of several corneal diseases that produce visually disabling opacities. "Cat OD" is shorthand for the presence of a cataract of the right eye.

Cavanagh told Sargus Houston that he had a cataract and a bad cornea and needed surgery. Houston agreed. Dr. Martin, his Macon doctor, had told him he could trust Dr. Cavanagh, that he would do right by him. Houston had faith.

Cavanagh further wrote "Plan—PK+ECCE+PC IOL OD, elective," meaning he planned to do his triple. He walked Houston to the side office, where his secretary scheduled the surgery for September, the soonest date available.

* * *

JUNE 1983

Every June, the eye faculty looked forward to their annual retreat. This year they would meet at Callaway Gardens. Only a ninety-minute drive from Atlanta, the facility provided a peaceful setting with activities for young families. The past few retreats had allowed the department to review its considerable accomplishments and plan for more. The department was cohesive and proud.

For David Campbell, however, doubts, worries, and anxieties had eroded his sense of well-being and pride. He had talked to Cavanagh, written a letter, and had seen no results, no lessening of patient volume. Dr. Campbell didn't know that Allen Gammon had spoken with Cavanagh; Campbell had his own worries and knew that rumors were beginning to circulate in the community. George Waring, aware of problems, did not talk with Cavanagh and, in a later letter, he frankly admitted being afraid of Dr. Cavanagh.

Why should Waring, or any of the faculty, be afraid? The eye department had all witnessed the retaliation Cavanagh attempted to visit upon Dr. Frank Bell, the third of the Three Musketeers, when he left the faculty to practice in town. In my interview with him, Frank Bell related that he had decided to practice at St. Josephs Hospital to develop a retinal practice complete with a surgical team. One day, as Bell was at the hospital checking on preparations for his arrival, he saw another Emory retinal surgeon leaving the hospital administrator's office. Bell learned that Dwight Cavanagh had sent this doctor to pursue setting up a retina service run by Emory, thus thwarting Bell's plans. Bell went to Charles Hatcher, and the idea was cancelled.

An academic chairman, like any boss, wields power. The chair awards salaries, academic rank, grant endorsements, secretarial and other support, lab space—in short, all the necessities in a teaching center. Dwight Cavanagh was already known as of one of the most powerful chairmen on the Emory campus. For whatever reasons, with the exception of Campbell and Gammon, each individual faculty member had been silent on the subject of Dwight Cavanagh's overextended practice.

But the Cavanagh problem festered in Campbell. He felt he could not keep his self-respect if he did not act, no matter the consequence. He and Cavanagh had remained friends in the early 1980s.

Even though Campbell's warning in August had yielded no result, Campbell thought another, more public warning should not greatly strain their relationship.

In these times, my relationship with David Campbell had grown. I had continued to teach at the Emory glaucoma clinic at Grady every other week, attended the weekly grand rounds (teaching conference attended by faculty, residents, fellows and local ophthalmologists), and held a clinical appointment on the Emory faculty. Dr. Campbell and I consulted on difficult patients with each other and participated in clinical research studies together. Even though we were not at Grady together, our friendship had increased over the years.

About this time, I had called David Campbell about a patient, a seven-year-old child, whom Cavanagh had scheduled for corneal transplantation even though the eye was perfectly normal. This child was a patient of one of my partners in my practice group. My partner had referred the child to Dr. Cavanagh and had received the usual written report. Cavanagh's letter confirmed that the eye had recovered as expected from a self-limited condition. But Dr. Cavanagh had scheduled the child for a corneal transplant and, contrary to custom, had not reported this to my partner. When my partner accidentally heard about the scheduled surgery from the mother, he re-examined the child, found a normal cornea, and told the family to cancel the surgery. It would be unconscionable to put a child through such an unneeded operation.

Corneal transplantation in the early 1980s was a far-from-perfect operation. The suturing techniques caused large amounts of astigmatism, and many eyes never regained normal vision. Add to this the many postoperative visits, the need for prolonged eye-drop treatments, the lifelong risk of graft rejection, and you had an operation that should be done only when necessary, when a patient's vision was greatly reduced. This was especially true for children who were more difficult to follow after transplant surgery.

Several weeks before the retreat, Campbell invited Gammon into his office. Allen Gammon and David Campbell, very different in personalities and styles, had not been close. They respected each other professionally but had different friends and social lives. As Gammon sank into the chair, David Campbell launched right in, and they began to discuss the problems each of them had observed.

Gammon described a two-year-old child with a previously transplanted cornea, who had been operated on by Cavanagh. The child had reported back to Gammon with a corneal ulcer, an eye emergency and a sight-threatening condition without prompt treatment. Gammon arranged for a visit with Cavanagh and went about his business. A few weeks later, the child reappeared in Gammon's office. The eye was blind, and Cavanagh had never carried out any treatment. Gammon was greatly upset.

The two then discussed the rumors circulating amongst the fellows and residents about aggressive surgery and chart alterations. Gammon didn't tell David Campbell, but Gammon had decided to take his concerns to Charles Hatcher. David Campbell continued his plans to speak up at the retreat.

During the retreat, Dr. Campbell addressed his partners, now numbering at least ten, who were assembled in the meeting room. Their chairman was too busy—too busy on his clinic days and too busy in the operating room. Now the community was beginning to know about it and express concern. Their reputations were at stake.

As Campbell continued, everyone heard his concerns, including Dwight Cavanagh. As frequently happens in a public meeting, the culture of politeness prevailed. Campbell did not mention the specific, damning details, just his general concerns of long patient waits and the potential for mistakes. The message was delivered but in a diluted manner. Not surprisingly, no one else spoke a word, and nothing changed. The train kept going, seemingly still on the tracks.

* * *

JUNE 1983

Genevieve Switz had been Cavanagh's physician assistant for three weeks. She had recently finished Emory's Physician Assistant Program, graduating with a degree of Bachelor of Medical Science in December 1982. This was her first job after a lot of schooling, and she was anxious to do well.

Cavanagh had hired her to assist him with patient care. She was to perform admission histories and physicals and help with medical management and preoperative education on his patients. In addition, she assisted him at some of his surgery and helped with the postoperative care of his patients.

Switz had enjoyed the first few weeks of her new job, but she had noticed a practice pattern that puzzled her. She took her concern to Dr. Alan Kozarsky, still a cornea fellow, who would shortly complete his training and become a faculty member in the eye department. She had noted that African-American patients were all operated on at the end of the day. Was her observation accurate?

Kozarsky told her that it wasn't just the African-American patients; it was the poor white ones as well. That was the type of patient Cavanagh let fellows operate on while he assisted and taught them surgical technique.

But fellows only got to operate at the end of the day, so they just learned to put them last. Dr. Cavanagh had the last word on the schedule anyway, and he would put them at the end if the fellow didn't. They all wanted to operate, too, so that was how they got it done.

Switz had already seen that doctors in training, whether residents or fellows, wanted to do surgery themselves, and getting their own cases consumed them. Most patients who come to an academic medical center know that they will spend a certain amount of their time seeing students, residents, or fellows. Many fewer realize that these young doctors perform part and sometimes all of their procedures, both diagnostic and surgical, under supervision of the full-time faculty. In the case of Cavanagh's service, as Dr. Kozarsky would later testify, the custom was to put the "poor, unconnected" patients last, and the reward was that the fellow got the surgical experience. In Georgia in the 1980s this meant many of these patients were African-American, although the differentiation was economic, not racial.

Kozarsky's answer did not placate Switz. She began keeping copies of the daily surgical schedules, noting which patients were African-American and where in the rotation their surgery was performed. She kept these records at home. She also kept records and portions of the charts of patients with untoward outcomes. She could not know how important these records would become or the eventual cost to her for keeping them.

* * *

LATE JUNE 1983

Allen Gammon, frustrated by his unproductive meeting with Dr. Cavanagh a few months earlier, had taken his worries to Dr. Charles Hatcher. He and Dr. Hatcher had met right before the retreat, and Hatcher had listened intently, occasionally commenting. In his deposition, Gammon related that he told Hatcher about the infant's eye lost to the corneal ulcer. And Hatcher responded, "You win some and you lose some." Then Gammon had complained about the lack of support from Cavanagh, and Hatcher had responded, "That's an issue you have to fight on your own. I can't help you." Gammon had questioned Cavanagh's mental status as he had laid out his concerns.

Allen Gammon never dreamed how quickly the word would reach his chairman. Late one afternoon after the retreat, Dr. Gammon was discussing a mutual patient with Dwight Cavanagh. To Gammon's surprise, Cavanagh brought up the meeting with Hatcher. According to Gammon's later deposition, Dr. Cavanagh said that Gammon had made a big mistake, talking to Charlie Hatcher, criticizing his practice and even questioning Cavanagh's sanity. That was dumb, plain old dumb. Gammon had better hear this loud and clear: Cavanagh's support for him was finished.

Nothing that Gammon said could mollify Cavanagh. The fact that Gammon was the first ever to go above Cavanagh's head especially angered him. During the coming months he would face payback and the consequences of losing his chairman's support. As Hatcher had told him, he was on his own. But Gammon wasn't a quitter. Giving up was simply not in his nature.

* * *

JULY 1983

Dr. Philip Newman, Dwight Cavanagh's cornea fellow for the next three months, began learning the details of Cavanagh's service even before his starting date of July 1. Newman thought he knew something about Emory and being a fellow. He had already served a valuable year in Emory's research lab after completing a prestigious fellowship in medical diseases of the cornea in San Francisco. He blinked frequently behind thick glasses. His blinking, combined with a furrowed brow, gave him a bewildered look and caused some people to underestimate his abilities.

Newman discovered that Cavanagh, unlike the other cornea doctors, handled the assignment of corneal tissue to the transplant patients for the day himself. Corneal tissue comes from the Eye Bank, whose technicians "harvest" corneas from recently deceased patients. The younger the patient and the fresher the tissue, the better the recipient eye does. An important advance in corneal-transplant surgery was the invention of a solution that kept corneal tissue fresh for days. With that invention, corneal transplantation was changed from an emergency surgery performed at odd hours to a scheduled procedure during normal daily times. Still, the younger and fresher, the better, and the Eye Bank technicians graded tissue on appearance and other factors.

Some corneal surgeons took only the best tissue and would cancel surgery if a certain grade was unavailable. Others, including Cavanagh, would use all grades allowable, all but the clearly unusable tissue. After all, if tissue was below a certain grade, it could not be used. Switz would later testify that Cavanagh handled the grading issue by using the best first. Thus, all factors being equal, those receiving operations early in the day had the best statistical chance of retaining their grafts and seeing clearly. Switz remembered a day when Cavanagh moved a Coca-Cola executive from number six on the schedule to first.

Another unusual feature of Cavanagh's service involved chart dictation. Cavanagh insisted on dictating operative reports himself, a practice highly unusual in academic medicine. Almost every doctor who has a physician as an assistant assigns the task of dictation to the helper. Dictating takes time, and time becomes more precious the more senior the physician is. The fellows and Cavanagh's fellow faculty marveled at the sight of him hunched over the charts, not only dictating but also filling out billing slips. Many faculty have no clue about medical-practice finances; Cavanagh made sure every charge was entered correctly.

Dr. Newman had conferred with Switz, now the most experienced member of the Cavanagh team with all of five weeks behind her. She relayed what she had learned from Alan Kozarsky: Keep things moving; speed counts. Have the patients ready for surgery, all testing done, all clearances from internal medicine and anesthesia accomplished, no delays. Dr. Cavanagh handled the assignment of tissue and would rearrange the order of patients if Newman didn't get it right. Cavanagh dictated, but Newman would do the handwritten note in the chart. And he didn't like to see fellows mention complications in that written note, not even the big ones. Just do it his way. Again, speed counts. Dr. Cavanagh, no prima donna, had actually mopped the floor between cases himself to move things along. So don't slow things down.

* * *

AUGUST 1983

Dr. Bob Allen, David Campbell's new glaucoma partner, had never seen a patient this angry. He had just told this man, a Cavanagh patient referred to Allen for glaucoma evaluation, that his left eye was 70% blind. The patient was forty-three years old, an executive with Georgia Power, intense and compulsive about everything. Allen's stool moved farther and farther away as the words blistered him.

The man, unlike many of Cavanagh's patients, had picked up on things right away. He took in that the tests performed by Bob Allen had never been done before, that the diagnosis of glaucoma mentioned by Dr. Allen was a new one, that the discovery of significant vision loss was made today, not previously, despite years of appointments with Cavanagh. He was not happy. Why hadn't tests been done before? Treatment started? Treatment could have prevented permanent loss of his vision.

Allen sighed, sliding his stool to the desk, and picked up the chart. But he didn't need to look in the chart; he had seen too many of them already. It was always the same—high pressures measured by the technicians or residents crossed out by Cavanagh and lower pressures written in or the notation "FT soft," or "finger tension soft," meaning the eye's pressure felt normal when Cavanagh pressed his index finger on the eye. No mention of the optic nerve or the peripheral vision, no tests done, no treatment. No hint from the chart that anything was amiss. Yet these patients had lost vision frequently, a lot of vision. And they obviously had advanced glaucoma damage when Allen saw them, damage that took months or years to develop.

So what do you say to the patient? Allen's thoughts were: *My chairman blew it; he missed your disease; sorry you're blind, but it's too late now. Instead of paying attention to the pressure recorded by his assistants and giving you some drops to keep you from going blind, he crossed out the numbers he didn't like, put his fingers on your eye, even though they quit doing that years and years ago, and wrote that the pressure was normal. So now your eye is blind and it didn't need to be. And I've seen so many like you already, I'm sick and half crazy.* But, he couldn't express these thoughts to a patient.

So the story would go something like this: Mr. Wade, your eye pressure is high and you have some nerve damage. Part of your side vision is lost, but you have a good bit left. Glaucoma sometimes occurs after a corneal transplant, and it can be very sneaky and very tricky to detect in the early stages. Pressure fluctuates and can be up and down in the same day. But then it gets more obvious and can be diagnosed. And we do have treatment, usually eye drops, and drops are all most people need. There is also laser treatment and, as a last resort, surgery.

Allen couldn't tell the patient that he had gone to Cavanagh several times and written memos, begging Cavanagh to do more visual field testing and to send him the patients sooner, before damage occurred. Allen had even gotten Mary Gemmill, Cavanagh's main technologist, to go ahead and order testing based on her suspicions. He had done all he could do as junior faculty to remedy the situation. But the patients kept coming, and Cavanagh's neglect festered in Allen's conscience.

CHAPTER FOUR

THE OPERATION

SEPTEMBER 1983

Sargus Houston felt fine, but his doctors didn't. They worried about him. Houston had entered the hospital on Sunday, September 11. The preoperative evaluation revealed that he had several medical problems. His blood pressure was too high and his blood potassium too low, making it dangerous in case he needed to be put to sleep. His blood count was low, and his heart had an irregular beat.

On Monday, the day of Houston's planned surgery, the anesthesiologist confronted Dr. Phil Newman between cases. He wanted to cancel Houston's surgery, postpone it while the medical team evaluated Houston further. It was their job to make sure patients lived through surgery, especially elective surgery. A few days' delay couldn't make much difference to Houston's sight, and surgery today could be dangerous.

Philip Newman felt stuck. He knew the right thing to do was cancel the case, but that would anger Cavanagh. They were doing thirteen cases that day, a huge caseload, but every case was crucial to the chief. Newman knew he couldn't make that decision; he had to check with the boss.

Dr. Cavanagh was not happy, but he devised a simple solution. They had good donor tissue; they weren't going to cancel. Call the case an emergency and move it to the last of the day. That would give them hours to fix his medical condition. If a case is an emergency, there is more leeway to operate on a marginally stable patient.

The day progressed uneventfully until after the twelfth case, when Charles Hatcher summoned Cavanagh to an emergency meeting. Dressed in scrub clothes, hat on with mask dangling, Cavanagh leaned forward at an especially acute angle as he sped into Hatcher's office.

What was going on? Dr. Cavanagh had done twelve cases that day and wasn't through. The operating room was waiting. Everyone wanted to go home. As Hatcher began, Cavanagh slumped in his chair, stunned. Hatcher wanted Cavanagh to fire Robert Wayne (pseudonym), Cavanagh's chief fund-raiser. Wayne had to go.

Cavanagh tried to take in this news. It was a bombshell. Robert Wayne was his mainstay for raising money. The new eye center was well on its way, and Cavanagh had almost reached the goal of raising $10 million dollars (equivalent to $22 million in 2008). Now they wanted to take away the man Cavanagh relied on to make it happen. After arguing and discussing with Hatcher, Cavanagh realized he had lost this round. His reaction, as he later related, was, "Now, without Mr. Wayne, no money; without money, no department."

Cavanagh sped back to the OR. He replaced his shoe covers, hat, and mask, and after scrubbing his hands and arms, he sat at the head of the bed, the anesthesiologist to his right. He always had the anesthesiologist sitting by the eye to be operated on. Thus the fellow could position himself on the other side, and Cavanagh would have plenty of room to work.

The physician's assistant entered the room. "Genevieve, block that eye," commanded Cavanagh as soon as he saw her. Still upset over his new financial problem, he motioned to the left eye. Switz, now a veteran of several months, later testified that she had learned never to cross or question Cavanagh. She, like the fellows and residents, had experienced his quiet but withering disapproval following any departure from his instructions.

She testified that she wanted to follow her routine and check the operative permit one last time, but he motioned to the left eye again. "Come on. Let's go." Assuming the surgeon knew his business, she complied.

A few minutes later, Dr. Newman entered the room, noted that Cavanagh was operating on the left eye despite the room's arrangement for a right-eye operation, and, despite some discomfort, began his part of the operation. Newman later testified that he wondered if the correct eye was being operated on, but it was late, he was tired, and he assumed that Dr. Cavanagh was correct and that he, Newman, was wrong. He flipped over the cornea and punched out the donor button, only mumbling as Cavanagh complained about the poor dilation of the left eye. "Why isn't the damn pupil dilated?"

As Cavanagh turned over the last part of the case to Dr. Newman, he told his fellow to partially sew the lids together as well. Protecting the surface of a fresh corneal graft is vital to long-term success, and some eyes need the extra step of partial lid closure. Cavanagh did more lid surgery than most corneal surgeons, and he always dictated a separate op note. Newman complied, despite the fact that the chart said nothing about a lid problem and that Cavanagh's initial plan was to operate only on the right eye, not the lids. Cavanagh retreated to the surgeons' lounge to dictate the day's thirteen cases.

Phil Newman finished the lids on Sargus Houston at 7:00 PM, about the time Cavanagh completed his dictation. The evening nurse came to Dr. Newman, puzzled. She didn't do many eye cases and wanted to know the difference between "OD" and "OS," the abbreviations of the Latin for "right eye" and "left eye." She had noted that the operating schedule was for Houston's "OD"—his right eye—but they had all written "OS" (left eye) in writing up the actual surgery.

Dr. Newman blanched, reading and rereading the chart and the schedule. He sat down, staring at the chart, desperate to find some explanation. After a few minutes, he couldn't deny it. The nurse was correct. Houston had been scheduled for his OD, the right eye, but they had operated on the OS, the left eye, the good eye, the eye with minimal corneal disease and a vision of 20/25. They had committed the ultimate surgical blunder, operating on the wrong organ.

Newman panicked and ran to Switz. An explosion of emotion filled the room. Fear permeated everything—fear of telling Cavanagh, fear of being blamed.

Switz would later testify that she called her husband at home and told him, "It finally happened," referring to previous conversations with him where she had predicted, "Things were so rushed and hectic that it wasn't inconceivable that such a thing would happen."

Philip Newman knew he was one of those mechanisms. His eyes were blinking so fast it was amazing he could see. He and Switz were concerned about themselves and their careers at this point also. What do they do now? Who would tell Dr. Cavanagh? Who would tell the patient, and what would they say to him?

Switz shot right back. He and Dr. Cavanagh were the doctors. Newman had better let anesthesia know and one of them let Cavanagh know. Then decide who tells the patient.

As she was instructing Newman, she noted that he was changing the hospital chart, crossing out "right eye" and inserting "left eye." She asked him what he was doing. Newman looked up, still blinking. He was getting the chart right. Switz told him to stop. The page Newman was working on already had another doctor's note on it, not to mention that changing a chart in this way defied all malpractice seminars and was illegal.

Newman stopped and then reversed himself. He identified all the changes he made in the correct manner so that anyone reviewing the chart could see his changes. He did make necessary changes, those that told the nurses to put the postoperative drops in the correct eye. Newman also wrote a reminder that the unpatched eye had very poor vision and that Houston would need more help in getting around than the typical patient.

Next came the hard job, something he dreaded in the worst way. The anesthesiologist refused to go first. After a few moments to summon his courage, Newman went looking for Cavanagh. It was his job to tell the surgeon.

Newman found Cavanagh in the lounge. He thrust the chart into Cavanagh's hands, said "We need to operate on the other eye as soon as possible," turned, and fled into the dressing room.

Minutes later, the anesthesiologist confronted a mystified Cavanagh.

"Dwight," he said, "we have a problem, a big problem. You operated on the left eye. His good eye. You were supposed to do the right."

Dwight Cavanagh would relate the following to one of the committees investigating this incident:

There are about eighteen things in an operating room that makes that [operating on the wrong eye] not happen. One, you come in, the nurse asks you which eye you are there for. The second thing, if the block [local anesthetic] occurs in the [operating] room, which it sometimes does, or if it occurs in the waiting area, the nurse, Anesthesia, and everyone always asks the patient which eye you are there for.

Bear in mind, this man is awake. It's local. And bear in mind the nurse came in and the one who started the case stopped and left and then another one came in and picked up and she didn't know. The P.A. and Anesthesia stood there without looking at the chart. I mean, it's my responsibility not to have picked it up, but I would say that every fail-safe mechanism in an operating room that exists failed.

Cavanagh's deposition testimony related the following, after Phil Newman returned to the room:

And I turned to Dr. Newman, and I said, "What in the world happened?"

And he said, "At that time, I thought we were in the wrong place [wrong eye]."

And I said, "Why in the world didn't you tell me that you thought we were in the wrong place?"

And he said, "Well, I wasn't completely sure," or words to that effect...

Well, my response to that [was] *I was fairly upset. I didn't berate anyone or, you know, I have the attitude that the person in charge bears the responsibility. And I was in charge and it was my responsibility. And at that point in time, an error having been committed, it didn't do any good to start blaming people. That's not my style.*

As both Dr. Newman and Switz would later testify, he reassured them that he would handle things, that the main job was to take care of the patient, keep his eye in good shape. He made sure they knew to keep this quiet. Word would get out, but the less said by them the better.

The next morning Ms. Switz and Dr. Newman met on the eye floor of Emory University Hospital, floor 6D, to make rounds on the patients. Not a single nurse or assistant said anything about Houston. They could see the word was out: no talking about this.

After cleaning Sargus Houston's eye, Dr. Newman told him that they "had decided" to operate on his left eye instead of his right one. Houston had no questions; he trusted them.

As soon as they left Houston, Switz turned on Newman. She didn't like what she had heard. Dr. Newman, as she would later testify, told her that Dr. Cavanagh had called him at home the night before, had told Newman what to say, had given him specific instructions: "Tell him we decided to operate on the left eye." Dr. Newman was following orders and, in his later testimony, he confirmed Cavanagh had told him just what to say to Sargus Houston.

After all, Houston was Cavanagh's patient, not theirs. During this argument, they looked at the two charts, the hospital chart and Cavanagh's clinic chart. Switz remembered that Houston's left eye was healthy, making Dr. Newman's statement to the patient about needing to do the left eye even more troubling. She had looked at this man's chart yesterday. There was no mention of anything significantly wrong with that left eye.

After looking at both charts, she looked even harder at Newman. She thought they had agreed not to change the chart. Newman nodded his agreement. She showed him a note added to the hospital chart, which said "Cat OS, rough surface, consider canthoplasty."

She then looked at Houston's clinic chart, in which the diagnosis was changed from "Cat OD" to "Cat OS," with "OD" obliterated, not lined through, and "OS" substituted.

When Cavanagh finished his clinic chart for a surgical patient, it was copied twice. The original stayed in Cavanagh's office, one copy went to the hospital, and the second went to pathology. Someone in addition to Newman had made changes in each of the hospital and clinic charts, but different changes had been made in each one, and they were different from those Dr. Newman had made and reversed the night before. That mystery person had neglected to make them jibe with the corresponding copies. Dr. Newman and Genevieve Switz looked at each other, and Switz spoke first. She didn't like anything about this. Nothing good could come from this, and pretty soon the blame would be spread around.

Switz and Newman knew who was low on the totem pole at Emory and who might one day be blamed, despite Cavanagh's reassurances. They both made copies of the hospital and clinic charts, each of which had the alterations made by someone other than them, and took the copies home with them to store in safe places.

Switz took another step. She testified that, "I objected privately to Newman, to Dr. Newman, and I decided not to—you know, I decided to avoid the patient and family so as not to have to answer any questions. And I decided that I needed to consult an attorney... because I didn't have the impression that what was happening represented the facts, and I didn't want to be a party to dishonesty."

Dr. Dwight Cavanagh told the story in the following way. He said that, on the night of the surgery, he called Houston's sister in Macon, Carrie M. Davison:

I told her that Mr. Houston's—I told her we had a problem. I reassured her and I said, "I think Mr. Houston's eye is going to be all right. However, we didn't operate on the eye we intended to."

I told her the same thing that I later told him [Sargus Houston], *that I thought this would be all right. That there was no complication during his surgery, but that I was concerned about his general medical health and condition, that there were serious health questions on the horizon, that we were perhaps fortunate enough to have been able to do the surgery.... I also told her it was not our custom to operate on the better of the two eyes because when we operated on the better of two eyes, when one had a complication, a hemorrhage or infection, that one would, obviously, one didn't want to have that in the better eye.*

When Carrie Mae Davison gave her testimony regarding the phone notification from Dr. Cavanagh, she said, "He called me. He didn't tell me what he was calling for. He told me that the operation went well and he—Sargus—was back in the room."

When asked if Cavanagh told her they had operated on the left eye instead of the right, she stated, "He didn't say anything about [the] eye. He said the operation went well. He didn't tell me nothing about no eye."

And Sargus Houston, when asked by the attorney, testified to the following:

Q: *Do you remember talking to a doctor that night, September the 12th, the night of your surgery, about the wrong eye having been operated on?*
A: *I don't know whether it was that night or not, but he told me they operated on the wrong eye.... He said they wouldn't let him operate on the other one.*
Q: *Do you know who said that?*
A: *No. One of the doctors.*
Q: *When is the first time after your surgery that you remember talking to Dr. Cavanagh?*

Q: *When I told him that he operated on the wrong eye.*

Q: *That was Dr. Cavanagh you told that to.*

A: *That's who I remember it to be.*

Q: *Dr. Cavanagh was the first doctor you told that they had operated on the wrong eye.*

A: *Yes, sir. I took it to be him.*

Q: *You took it to be him?*

A: *Yes, sir.*

Q: *And it was Dr. Cavanagh that told you they wouldn't let him operate on the other eye.*

A: *Yes, sir.*

Sargus Houston, with a patched left eye, now viewed the world through a blurred right eye.

The news of Cavanagh's blunder ripped through the department, into every office, every lab, every examining room. By noon the day after, everyone knew, but no one talked publicly. Whispers ghosted behind closed doors, penetrating everywhere. The news was too juicy, too unprecedented, and too sensational to be kept from everyone's ears.

David Campbell had a hard time believing it. Since his plea at the previous summer's retreat for Cavanagh to slow down—a plea totally ignored by Cavanagh both at the meeting and later—several of the faculty had been distinctly cool to Campbell.

Three camps were slowly emerging in the eye department. The first camp, which Campbell later called the "club," was made up of Cavanagh and the two retinal surgeons—Henry Kaplan and Travis Meredith—both of whom supported Cavanagh unequivocally and unreservedly. The second camp agreed with Campbell, privately and publicly. Allen Gammon and Campbell comprised this camp. The third, the other seven, agreed with Campbell in private but feared Cavanagh's wrath and kept quiet in public.

Travis Meredith met up with Campbell in the hall to see if Campbell had heard the news. Dr. Meredith, the more junior of the retinal specialists, had arrived at Emory in 1979. He and Cavanagh had begun their residency at Johns Hopkins together, but military service had intervened for Meredith, and he fell two years behind. Tall, about 6'2", with closely cut black hair and erect posture, Meredith had kept the military appearance. He also kept a military attitude and respected his chief.

Campbell motioned Dr. Meredith into his office, asking if this meant that Cavanagh would have to go. Meredith said certainly not, not until they had heard all the facts, all sides of the story, and most important, heard what Cavanagh had to say. The two half discussed and half argued about the next steps. The positions taken would change slightly over the coming months, but only slightly.

Meredith's position: Dwight's the chairman. He needs and deserves our support. He is putting us on the map, creating a great department. Give him a chance. Support him.

Campbell's counter: Dwight's too busy and won't slow down, no matter what they say or how they try. He won't listen. This disaster was predictable. His poor reputation in town affects all of us in the department, and it won't be long before it spreads outside Atlanta. Campbell could support Dwight only if he made drastic changes in the way he practiced.

Finally, they arrived at a plan. At the upcoming faculty meeting, Dr. Campbell would move for a faculty investigation. Travis Meredith would second and support it. Dr. Cavanagh wouldn't like it, but David Campbell would stand by the results of the faculty study.

* * *

Sargus Houston stayed in the hospital for eleven days, far longer than needed to recover from eye surgery. Houston's niece in Atlanta, Dorothy Fuller, visited him almost daily. When she first saw him, she exclaimed over the bandage on the left eye and wondered why they did the left eye.

Houston didn't know, only that they had "decided" to do it. He assured his niece that Cavanagh was optimistic and happy with the progress of the left eye.

* * *

The eye faculty met three days after Houston's surgery. They wondered how Dr. Cavanagh would handle the discussion. Cavanagh meandered through the prepared agenda and said nothing about Sargus Houston until Gammon prodded him. After a sharp exchange, Cavanagh discussed the evening of Houston's surgery.

Cavanagh noted that all measures usually taken to avoid disaster had failed. He was let down at every step along the way. It was 6:00, and there was a new team of nurses and techs. They all knew how it was with the evening shift. These nurses knew nothing about eyes. It would have been nice if the fellow, Dr. Newman, had everything properly arranged so that when he walked into the room the correct eye was ready. And Newman had caused him other kinds of trouble. And he wasn't happy with Genevieve Switz either; it was her job to check the operative permit. It was a terrible day in other ways. But the surgeon was captain of the ship, so he had to take responsibility.

Cavanagh continued on, in theory accepting responsibility but, in fact, blaming others who he felt had let him down. Finally, David Campbell spoke up and moved that a committee investigate the whole issue—how it happened and how something like this could be prevented in the future.

The room was silent. No one moved. David Campbell, expecting the agreed-upon second, eyed Travis Meredith, who was looking toward Cavanagh, avoiding Campbell's gaze.

After another moment, Dr. Allen Gammon seconded the motion. Travis Meredith objected. He wanted support for the chairman, not a potentially divisive investigation.

Cavanagh, losing control of the meeting, appointed George Waring chairman of a quality-review committee.

Campbell had another question: was Cavanagh going to charge the patient for the surgery? Yes, the patient, or more accurately, Medicare, would be charged. Cavanagh had talked to the clinic's attorney, Hunter Allen, and he had advised charging. He had also strongly advised that no one talk about this case. The potential for publicity and lawsuits was real. Everyone was to keep quiet.

David Campbell was not mollified. He felt the patient should not be charged and wanted to know other details. Travis Meredith pointed out that patients are charged for heart surgery even if they die. Cavanagh, instead of answering, adjourned the meeting.

* * *

As George Waring headed home, he pondered Cavanagh's choosing him to be chairman of the quality-review committee, a dubious honor, especially since Dr. Waring was already overburdened with tasks. Waring and Cavanagh were cordial colleagues but not close socially or personally. Perhaps the reason was the joke Waring had played on Cavanagh when Waring was to be introduced to the ophthalmologists of Georgia. In my interview with him, Waring recounted how he had a friend place a call pretending to be an Atlanta police detective, telling Cavanagh that Waring had been arrested. After a number of frantic and frustrating phone calls to police headquarters by Cavanagh, Waring appeared at his door, infuriating his chairman. Perhaps it was the stripper dressed as a gorilla in the clinic on Waring's fortieth birthday, a gorilla that chased a terrified Cavanagh into his office. Whatever the reason, they were not close.

In my interview, Waring's thoughts hearkened back a few years to one of the few occasions he and Cavanagh had spent time together alone. They were sitting on the porch of Cavanagh's beautiful home, smoking cigars and talking. Between puffs, Cavanagh said, "George, I am the most powerful ophthalmologist in the country" and listed the reasons. He was chairman of the National Eye Institute Council, which made final decisions about research grants to academic ophthalmologists across the country. He was secretary-treasurer of ARVO, the Association for Research in Vision and Ophthalmology, the premier research organization in ophthalmology. He had a leadership position in the American Academy of Ophthalmology. And the Emory Eye Center, one of the few such centers in the country at that time, was well on the way to completion, with all the necessary funds raised.

Now, with this new committee assignment, Dr. Waring was under the gun. Perhaps Cavanagh thought he could control him, especially since Cavanagh had persuaded Emory University to defend Waring in a lawsuit that was still under way. Waring and others had been sued over a restraint-of-trade issue involving a new type of eye surgery, radial keratotomy. He remembered telling himself that night on his way home, "Look out."

* * *

As Dr. Bob Allen, the second glaucoma specialist, left the faculty meeting, he ran into Phil Newman. Ignoring Cavanagh's warning, he pulled Dr. Newman into his office. He told Newman a few details of the faculty meeting, most importantly that Cavanagh had implied that Phil Newman had started the operation.

Newman recoiled in horror. No, no. He wasn't even in the operating room when the case started. When he came in, Cavanagh was already cutting out the button. Newman figured that Cavanagh had somehow changed his mind without letting Newman know, so Newman just set about doing his part of the surgery.

Newman wanted to know exactly what Cavanagh had said, but Bob Allen couldn't recall each word. Dr. Allen just knew the clear implication: Newman was to blame.

Newman trembled all the way to the parking lot. He barely found his car. Genevieve Switz was right. Cavanagh would shovel blame all around. And as the cliché goes, the bad stuff flows downhill. Newman was at the bottom of the hill, the lowest doctor around.

CHAPTER FIVE

INVESTIGATION: 1983–1984

SEPTEMBER 1983

Cavanagh had appointed George Waring as head of the quality-review committee, and it had to be set up right. It had to be protected from lawyers and others. Cavanagh and Waring had been through a legal nightmare already, one that had yet to end. They knew all the ropes and the need to protect information from the eyes of attorneys.

Several years earlier, when radial keratotomy (RK)—a procedure to change the shape of the cornea and allow nearsighted people to "throw away" glasses—was new, Waring had pioneered a study to be sure it would be safe for patients to undergo. Then and now, any surgeon in the country could try any new operation he wanted, as long as the patient could be talked into being a guinea pig and the hospital allowed it. Federal regulations for evaluating new surgical procedures do not exist as they do for new drugs.

Even though RK was considered cosmetic in nature and was not covered by insurance policies, Waring succeeded in obtaining a nationwide moratorium on RK procedures until he and his academic colleagues at Emory and centers around the nation could study the operation. They would perform the operation in a uniform manner and follow the patients carefully, noting the success rate as well as complications. If RK proved to be safe and effective, then any surgeon trained in the technique would be able to go ahead, but not until the study was completed. A lover of acronyms, Waring dubbed the study "PERK"—Prospective Evaluation of Radial Keratotomy.

A number of pioneer surgeons in private practice—who had already begun profiting from performing RK—sued Waring personally, Emory, and other academic centers for restraint of trade. Dr. Cavanagh had helped Waring through the legal quagmire, but Waring had suffered greatly, and it wasn't over. He still needed Cavanagh and Emory's help to bring this to a close and avoid personal loss.

Lawsuits traumatize doctors, as I well know. A patient sued me after I prescribed a higher-than-normal dose of cortisone for two weeks. Even though this had nothing to do with her eventual outcome, the insurance company strongly urged me to settle for $15,000. I complied, even though it rankled me to do so.

Waring appointed Dr. Travis Meredith and Dr. Doyle Stulting to his quality-review committee, hired an attorney from the prestigious law firm of King and Spalding, and set about the process of officially registering the committee on campus. It would soon be known simply as the Waring Committee.

When Dr. Stulting told Allen Gammon of his appointment to the committee, Gammon snorted. That was great. At a later time, Gammon would state that the three committee members were all bought and paid for. Cavanagh had just made Dr. George Waring a full professor; Dr. Meredith was already Cavanagh's strong ally, and Stulting was a junior member of the cornea team and had been at Emory just over one year.

Despite his displeasure with the makeup of the committee, Allen Gammon prodded George Waring almost weekly for action. When would they see results? What was going on?

Gammon would later testify that, initially, Waring told Gammon to lay off, that Waring saw little evidence of problems. But after only a few weeks, Waring had apologized, telling Gammon there were a lot of problems but that he needed time to gather the charts and do things right.

Dr. Waring sent word that he wanted to meet with Phil Newman. Dr. Newman insisted that all doors be closed and then began pacing. Newman was terrified, so petrified that he occasionally couldn't start his car, afraid of a bomb. Newman had heard all the rumors blaming him for the mistake in the Houston operation. This was his last year of training, and he was looking for a job. Who would hire him now?

Waring heard Dr. Newman's version of events and then reassured him. This meeting wasn't to flog Newman; it was to hear about events and ask Newman's help. Waring wanted all charts where Cavanagh had made changes or operated inappropriately. Dr. Newman was to bring them to Waring and no one else.

Newman left the meeting relieved. Perhaps recriminations and punishment were not in his future. Someone in authority was listening. He couldn't know it, but this would be the only time Dr. Newman had the opportunity to tell his story to Waring's committee.

* * *

OCTOBER 1983

Gladys Wilson had barely slept since the visit in July when Cavanagh had recommended the same operation for her right eye— the triple—that had blinded her left eye. Despite her misgivings, she had scheduled the operation for December, the earliest time on Cavanagh's schedule. As the weeks wore on, she couldn't stop thinking or talking about it.

Finally she found Dr. Alexander Ayres in Decatur. Ayres had finished the Emory eye program several years earlier and established a successful solo practice.

"And Dr. Cavanagh paints the prettiest picture for me, Dr. Ayres. He says I'll be driving a car and everything will be roses if I get my right eye done." Mrs. Wilson had to have another opinion. What did Dr. Ayres think? Ayres didn't know where to begin. He saw only a cataract in her right eye, no corneal problem and no need for a transplant.

Leaning back in his chair, Ayres told the truth as diplomatically as he could. Gladys Wilson transferred her care to Ayres, a burden off her mind for the first time in months.

A few weeks later, Ayres performed a standard cataract surgery with lens implantation. Wilson did well, recovering 20/20 vision in this one eye promptly. Her left eye remained a problem, so much so that she wouldn't drive for a long time. The ordeal at Emory had scarred her, and she brooded every day. She had had four operations; she had lost her eye; and she had not been treated well.

* * *

Late in the day, David Campbell heard footsteps go by his office several times. Finally there was a knock at the door, and Dr. Bob Allen, a rare visitor, entered. Although the two comprised the glaucoma service for Emory, they had minimal contact and separate practices. Dr. Campbell saw few of Dwight Cavanagh's patients, whereas Bob Allen saw most of them.

Allen had seen too much and had to share the worries that were beginning to consume him. Allen spilled out all the frustrations of the blind eyes he was seeing—glaucoma not diagnosed, and worse, pressures crossed out and charts altered.

He told Campbell about the observant and astute glaucoma fellow they were training this year. After seeing a number of Cavanagh's blinded eyes, the fellow had devised a new term: the "Cavanagh syndrome." The "Cavanagh syndrome" was a transplant patient blind from glaucoma with a clinic chart that had no hint of any problem; not a hint except perhaps crossed-out high pressures taken by the tech. It was a hell of a thing for a fellow to say about the chairman. Allen slumped in his chair. He had taken a risk, but he could keep quiet no longer.

Allen, relieved that David Campbell was a friendly audience, unloaded more of his heartaches. The chairman was supposed to show the faculty the highest quality, not the worst. Dr. Allen had come to Emory because of Cavanagh and his leadership. He was bitterly disappointed.

Dr. Allen had written Cavanagh memos about the missed glaucoma patients, talked to him, and even gotten the tech to order tests on her own. He didn't know what else he could do. The charts were worthless as far as being a medical record, and it was getting more obvious.

And what would their fellow say about Emory when he went off to be faculty at another university? That the Emory faculty knew about the problems but sat back and did nothing? What if someone sued Cavanagh and Dr. Allen had to testify? He worried that he would have to testify under oath and say that the two had discussed all the damaged eyes. Then what would Allen say, that his only action was to write a memo?

After reassuring Allen that the senior faculty, not Allen, had obligations in this matter, Dr. Campbell sought out Dr. Waring, only to find that he was gone for ten days. This was no surprise; Waring's speaking and research meetings had taken him out of the office for a total of 128 days in 1983. Soon after Waring returned, Campbell cornered him in his office, wanting to know what was happening with the investigation. It had been a month since Waring was appointed chairman.

Waring replied as he had before: Lawyer keeps delaying. Waring was busy. Writing a book. Writing journal articles. Giving talks. Getting married. He was working on it.

Dr. Campbell told Waring about Bob Allen's revelations. They weren't news to Waring. Waring related a story he had just heard: The tech sees a Cavanagh patient the night before surgery and measures a pressure of 52, extremely high. Cavanagh records 20.

Dr. Stulting confirms the 52, tells Cavanagh no way he should do a transplant with pressures that high, and Cavanagh agrees. The next day he operates anyway. And that was just this month, right after he did the wrong eye. (Author's note: This patient later sued Dr. Cavanagh.)

Dr. Waring assured Campbell the committee work would be done. Bigger questions bothered Waring. What would be done with the report once it was ready? Would anybody do anything?

* * *

DECEMBER 1983

Barney Chisholm, the chief financial officer for the Emory Clinic, had a happy mission this month. He was delivering bonus checks to Charles Hatcher's big producers on campus. Dr. Hatcher had a particularly big bonus for Cavanagh—$250,000 ($552,000 in 2008). This bonus was more than twice the amount received by anyone else in the department and far more than Cavanagh had received before.

Clinic finances were somewhat of a mystery to almost all Emory doctors. They received multiple checks, one from Emory University and several from the clinic. Monthly drawing accounts, bonus checks, "40 percent" checks—all were welcome, but few knew how the sums were derived. Cavanagh, Hatcher, and Chisholm decided bonus amounts for the various faculty under Cavanagh; Hatcher alone decided the section chiefs'. Not all section chiefs received largesse this generous, but many did, and they remained quite loyal to the giver, Charles Hatcher. Cavanagh did not have to feign surprise; he had no idea his check would be this large.

At the same time, Chisholm may have had a warning for Cavanagh as well. The department's overhead expenses were up, and the eye faculty needed to cut back. These expenses could become a problem as the year wore on.

* * *

JANUARY 1984

George Waring's extensive travel schedule forced him to work on weekends when he was in Atlanta. One cold January day, Waring, coffee cup in one hand and a briefcase full of papers in the other, saw Dr. Bob Allen in the hall. Waring told Allen he had been meaning to talk to him about Cavanagh's neglected glaucoma patients.

Allen, index finger to his mouth to shush Waring, ushered him into his office and shut the door. Allen repeated what he had told David Campbell and then challenged Waring. What were they doing? It had been months. Nothing had changed. Waring threw up his hands and went through the litany of excuses. The current best one was that Georgia law was changing in March, making committee actions after that date even more impregnable to prying plaintiff's attorneys and reporters. They had to wait until then to register the committee. Right now, Waring was a one-man committee, gathering charts and talking to people. But nothing official could be done.

When Dr. Allen told Waring of the many altered charts he had seen, Waring told him of charts from Cavanagh's patients that showed charges for removal of membranes during corneal transplant surgery. The diseases that were being treated couldn't possibly have had a membrane needing removal; membranes simply didn't exist in those types of problems.

Bob Allen wasn't finished. He told Dr. Waring that Dwight Cavanagh's quality of care worried Allen greatly. Waring left the office hearing yet another plea to hurry up and do something; and not just something, the right thing. Bob Allen needed a role model he could look up to.

* * *

FEBRUARY 1984

Dr. Cavanagh operated on Sargus Houston's second eye, the former bad eye, on February 20. Houston was the sixth of seven cases that day. Interestingly, no lid procedure was done, only the triple procedure of corneal transplantation, cataract extraction, and IOL implantation. Cavanagh had written in large bold lettering on Houston's clinic chart, "**NO WAIT. HDC ONLY**." He wrote on the next page, "**ACCEPT ASSIGNMENT**."

"Accept assignment" instructed the billing office to accept whatever Medicare and any insurance company paid as payment in full, never to send the patient a bill. The rest was clear. This patient was a VIP, and only HDC (Harrison Dwight Cavanagh) was to see him, and do not subject this patient to the usual four-to-six hour wait. The surgery proceeded uneventfully, and Houston went home on schedule on February 26.

Later in the month, President Laney promoted Charles Hatcher to vice president for Health Affairs. No longer did he share the title with John Palms. The promotion ratified the reality that had existed since the two were named co–vice presidents: Hatcher led everything related to health care on the Emory campus, the medical school, the hospital, and the medical school faculty. The Emory Clinic remained separate, but Dr. Hatcher kept his hand near the controls, even though another doctor had taken Hatcher's place as the CEO.

* * *

MARCH 1984

The warning from Barney Chisholm proved to be accurate. The ophthalmology department was in financial trouble and costs had to be reduced. Dwight Cavanagh fired Genevieve Switz. Before she left, she warned George Waring that he was holding on to charts too long. The more he waited to do something about the problems, the more outsiders would view the department as complicit in the affair. The department also fired one of Allen Gammon's secretaries. Cavanagh imposed other cost-cutting measures relating to travel and expenses, but he did not disclose the bonus he had received a few months earlier, nor did he return these dollars to the department.

* * *

MAY 1984

Bob Allen took David Campbell into his office late one afternoon when the patients and staff had gone. Allen was resigning, and he wanted Campbell to be the first to know. Dr. Allen was returning to his home state of Virginia. He repeated his reasons. Cavanagh represented poor quality, not the best, as Allen had previously thought. Dr. Cavanagh was deficient as a role model, on and on. Bottom line: Bob Allen would no longer have his name and reputation associated with this type of program. In his deposition, Allen Gammon provided another reason that Dr. Allen left: Allen told him that he refused to work for a sociopath. Bob Allen was the first casualty at the faculty level. Would others follow?

When Allen Gammon and Dr. Campbell discussed Bob Allen's departure, they noted that it had been eight months since Sargus Houston's surgery. The committee had just been registered and had never even met. Switz was fired, as was Gammon's secretary. Dr. Gammon was upset and frustrated.

Both Campbell and Gammon realized that the stakes were being elevated, that a serious situation was getting more so. Should they leave, follow Bob Allen out the door? Or should they stay and fight. What was it for these two? Neither planned nor wanted to leave Atlanta. Their families were settled; they liked the city and all it offered. Research prospects were great. The rest of the faculty was high quality, and the training program was growing in reputation. Emory was a leading university. Why should they leave?

Yet they were realists. Someone seemed to be protecting Cavanagh, not allowing any type of clinic or hospital investigation. An incident report had been filed at the time of the wrong-eye operation, but there had been no follow-up or official hospital action. People were being fired. Were they next? Should they get legal advice?

They resolved to stay, to struggle on. Gammon reported that he had bought a tape recorder. Henceforth, he would tape every meeting, every discussion. If they landed in court, he would have ammunition.

They discussed the rest of the faculty. Would anyone else leave? Gammon was sure not. Everyone was hunkered down, avoiding crossfire and hoping for a truce. The club was gaining power; the rest were cowering. None of them would leave.

No, the fight was Gammon's and Campbell's, theirs and theirs alone.

* * *

JULY 1984

Against the backdrop of faculty unrest, money-raising, eye-center construction, and chart reviews, patient care carried on. On July 17, Sargus Houston journeyed from Macon yet again. On his previous visit two months earlier, the tech measured his vision without glasses—and indeed he had no glasses yet—and indicated he had Counting Fingers vision—CF—in each eye, meaning he could see no letters on the chart and could only correctly count the number of fingers she held in front of his face.

She had performed a refraction, the act of measuring to see which combination of lenses would improve his vision. The right eye could see 20/50, but the correcting lenses were +4.00 + 5.00 x

105. The right eye was significantly farsighted and had astigmatism. When an eye has astigmatism, light is bent more in one direction than another and the compensating spectacle lens has to be curved much more in one direction than another.

The left eye, his former good eye, could only see the biggest *E* on the chart, the 20/400 *E*, and only with a similar degree of astigmatic correction. On paper, the overall vision was not bad, with one eye achieving 20/50 vision, but this report was deceptive. Had he been given glasses, they would have been expensive, difficult to adjust to, and likely to be changed by the next visit.

Fluctuating astigmatism commonly followed corneal transplantation, often for months after surgery. Visual rehabilitation dragged, especially with the suturing technique used by Cavanagh. He chose to use only one suture, "running" it for the entire 360 degrees. Doctors Waring, Stulting, and others in the department placed numerous individual sutures in addition to a running suture. With this newer technique, a single suture could be cut and high amounts of astigmatism relieved. This second technique took more time and, for whatever reason, Cavanagh chose to use one suture.

Now in July, Houston was doing better. "Doing pretty good," came the stock reply. In fact, his vision had improved, 20/40 now in the formerly bad right eye. The eye that had been incorrectly operated on continued to see poorly, partly from wound irregularity and partly from haziness from a membrane behind his lens implant. Dwight Cavanagh recorded the pressure in this eye as 21, borderline for glaucoma.

Mattie Brown saw Cavanagh that month as well. She complained that he had operated on her eye two years ago, with her son Gerald bringing her back and forth from Calhoun for many visits. Yet she still couldn't see from the eye, and it bothered her every day.

Instead of his stock, "Hang in there, Mattie," Cavanagh offered a solution. He told Brown that the cornea had "slipped" and needed an operation to correct it. Then she would get that good eye he had promised her.

On the trip back to Calhoun, she dissolved into tears, just as she did after every visit. Gerald tried to console her. At least he was going to do something. Did he say what was wrong, why he had to go back to the operating room? Between sobs, she managed that he was always moving, always on the go. He had just told her that something slipped.

Cavanagh repaired her graft on July 23, 1984. She went home the same day no better, eye hurting and blurred.

Eight days later, the following memo announced a long-awaited vacation for Cavanagh:

MEMO TO All Clinical Full-Time Faculty
FROM H. Dwight Cavanagh, M.D. DATE 7-31-84

Gentleman [sic]*:*
In departing for vacation today, just before the small man with the butterfly nets comes to get me, I would like to share with you a few disjointed thoughts.

First, I am very proud of all of you. And I want to express my appreciation to each of you for all you have done and are continuing to do on behalf of our mutual efforts. We have held together over a period of many years under conditions that have been simply frightful. Those conditions and the stress of growth and competition have placed a great burden on all of us. I have come to rely more and more on periods of solitude and recovery, and I hope and trust each of you will find some time away this summer to recharge your batteries for the remaining struggles ahead. This time away is not merely desirable to the life and mind of the human spirit.

November should see a culmination of our efforts and a solution to many of the day-to-day stresses that plague all of us. The [new eye center] building is not an end in itself, however. It is an opportunity. As I see it, it is a chance to put us all together so that we can interact more meaningfully with mutual support for professional and personal growth. Life, after all, is like a train journey through mountains, prairies, days, nights, and struggles. We tend to concentrate on the goals—where the train station is and when we will arrive. Punctuated along the way are a series of small stops and platforms. Dedication of the new building will be one such platform. The real meaning and purpose of this accomplishment is not in the bricks and mortar and is not in the dedication, as life is not in the station or the goals. The purpose is the journey, the interaction between each of us that allows for meaningful group process leading to personal awareness and growth. Somehow we are all bound together in the journey, and it will not be long before the final station is to come.

Take care of yourselves. See you after Labor Day.

Dwight

Dr. Cavanagh was correct. Struggles remained. While the chairman recharged his batteries on the South Carolina beach, Dr. Waring and Dr. Stulting threw themselves into intensive chart reviews, totaling several hundred. They invaded Cavanagh's office as well; his secretary surrendered a huge number of charts.

* * *

SEPTEMBER *1984*

In mid-September, Cavanagh escorted Sargus Houston into his office. As he had instructed the day after the surgery, Cavanagh was the only one to examine Houston. Houston wasn't the only worry for the chairman. He had attended a recent meeting of the Atlanta Ophthalmology Society. There, Dr. Clinton D. "Sonny" McCord, formerly on Cavanagh's faculty as the oculoplastic specialist, had taken Cavanagh aside and warned Cavanagh of rumors in town that Cavanagh was on his way out and would never move into the new building.

Cavanagh had bristled. He thought the whole world knew about Sargus Houston, and he assumed the rumors were associated with that surgery. But Cavanagh knew he would be moving into the center, even if he were the only one. Someone else had come up and interrupted them, and they hadn't pursued it further. But the warning resonated in Cavanagh's mind.

Dr. Cavanagh recorded in Houston's chart: "Comes in alone today, walks well, says he is doing well; TV, reading all fine. He is very happy and pleased."

He further recorded vision as 20/30 on the right and 20/200 on the left. He wrote that the pressures were 15 and 18, and the only abnormalities noted were some tight sutures on the left and some haze of the membrane behind the lens implant on the left.

Cavanagh instructed Houston to make an appointment for February, five months hence, and noted in the chart that he would consider cutting the tight sutures and performing a laser procedure on the hazy membrane then. Cavanagh could not know it, but this was the last time he would see Houston, at least in his examining room.

On the way back to Macon, Sargus' niece looked closely at her uncle. She was concerned about his vision. After observing how he navigated in and out of the clinic, she thought he saw poorly, but he said he was seeing well.

* * *

Later in September, George Waring convened the quality-review committee. He, Doyle Stulting, and Travis Meredith gathered to consider the next steps.

Waring reviewed with Meredith the results of the chart review performed by Waring and Stulting. Waring emphasized that they had performed only a review of charts, not a full-scale investigation with interviews of witnesses or patients. Waring warned of a "vigilante" attitude in the minds of some faculty, of faculty hiring attorneys, worried about their own legal liability. The department was teetering, waiting for their committee's report. Some people wanted to string Dwight up; others wanted exoneration. This affair could destroy the department.

Here were the issues determined from the chart review:

1. Wrong-eye surgery
2. Alteration of charts
3. Surgery on eyes for diseases that did not exist
4. Inappropriate early surgery for minimal disease
5. Multiple billings for procedures performed at same operation
6. Fraudulent billing for surgical procedures not performed
7. Inappropriate management of patients leading to severe loss of vision.

They had uncovered multiple examples of all the issues listed, except, of course, only one wrong eye operated on. The list spoke for itself and was unprecedented in academic medicine. Now what? Write it up and send it around? Call in Dr. Charles Hatcher? Call in the feds and fess up? Return the money? No, they needed to discuss it some more, to involve the rest of the faculty, at least the senior faculty. They should give Dr. Cavanagh the chance to explain these charges, see what he says. So they decided to meet with the senior, tenured eye faculty to discuss it with them and go from there.

George Waring had anticipated this decision and had already set up a meeting. He had made one mistake: inviting Allen Gammon. Dr. Meredith would hear none of this; he felt Gammon was nothing but trouble. Gammon was uninvited. Gammon didn't like it, but he did not have tenure and lacked the clout to force the issue.

October was showdown month.

* * *

Shortly after Waring's quality-review committee meeting, Cavanagh sent the following memo to his three colleagues in cornea:

PERSONAL & CONFIDENTIAL
DATE: September 27,1984
TO: Cornea Service Clinicians:
R. Doyle Stulting, M.D.
George O. Waring, M.D.
Louis A. Wilson, M.D.
FROM: H. Dwight Cavanagh, M.D.

I think several of you may be aware that during this past academic and fiscal year ending September 1 there has been a quietly desperate, life-and-death struggle to complete the financing, equipping, and occupancy of the new eye center without going under. During this period and for the past five years there has been a constant, always bitter fight on my part to prevent sequestration of operating income to be used for bricks and equipment, and to raise the necessary additional funds. By implementing this constant squeeze, the school literally placed us in direct jeopardy of bankruptcy. This battle is over. We have, for the moment, won.

In this war there has been some real blood shed and some casualties. I am one. It is very clear to me that I can no longer pay the personal, physical, and professional price of carrying the department clinically, nor am I willing to continue to do so. This is my ninth year here. I feel that I have earned some peace. The timing is right now; I would have done it sooner if I could. For me the continued stretching out of the necessity of this effort has been a personal Gethsemane. I am no longer willing to compromise myself in continuing it.

In order to achieve peace and sanity and be able to devote the necessary time to administration that the new eye center will require, I am going to reduce my clinical work to half a day per week, effective with building occupancy.... I really do not wish to operate at all; but, realistically, there are usually 4–5 old/new patients per month that probably will have to be done. These would include the V.I.P.s (trustees, N.W. Atlantans, Ellis Jones' mother (staff families), Senator Nunn's mother, etc., etc.) that are not only unavoidable, but necessary for fund-raising and community political purposes.... As all of you know, I do care deeply about my patients, as I care about you, and like to have a close personal relationship with them. At this point, however, I have to do either a good, full-time job of running the department or become a good, full-time outside clinician. You might be interested in knowing that not less than 3 of my patients told me this in clinic yesterday.

In order to facilitate discussion, I would like to point out the following problems that will need agreement:

1. *There are approximately 600–800 patients that need care....*

2. *By splitting up my practice and surgery, each of you can contribute to meeting this need; and, at the same time increase your salaries somewhere between $15,000 and $50,000 depending on who does what.... It probably will come to pass that several (or all) of you will end up with incomes greater than mine. So be it. If I were interested in money, I would long ago have gone across town and made millions. Over the past eight years, I have contributed $128,000/year (Chair Funds) X8= $1,024,000 to the department plus 4 million from clinical work. Enough is enough.*

To the extent that I am burned out and battered by this struggle, I will tell you that I harbor no personal bitterness or negative feelings toward anyone. I have done what I could, and given as much as I can for as long as I can. I have had some triumphs and I have had some disasters; made good decisions and some awful blunders; done things I ought not to have done and left undone many others I should have done—and now enough. My feelings are most closely summed up by the Greek, Cavafy:

Honor to those who in the life they lead
define and guard a Thermopylae. Never
betraying what they feel is right,
consistent and just in all they try to do
but showing pity also, and compassion;
generous when they are rich, and when they're poor,
still generous in the small ways,
still helping as much as they can;
always trying to speak the truth,
yet without hating those who lie.
And even more honor is due to them
when they foresee (as many do foresee)
that Ephialtis will turn up in the end
that the Medes will break through after all.

I look forward to meeting with you.

HDC

Within hours, Cavanagh's memo, intended for his three cornea colleagues only, had been copied and seen by almost every faculty member. Many openly laughed as they read and discussed it with varying degrees of disbelief and disgust. The meaning was clear. Cavanagh's share of the patients, and therefore more money, would now be coming to the three cornea doctors, all of whom would soon be judging him.

* * *

TUESDAY, OCTOBER 2, 1984
EMORY DENTAL SCHOOL

George Waring called the committee to order. This conference room would be their home for the next few nights. Sandwiches, chips, and cans of Coca-Cola stood off to the side of a long table. Dr. Waring had chosen an obscure location in the basement of the dental school for these meetings. He wanted total privacy; no one was to see this group gathering. He feared exposure and publicity.

Waring began by noting that this was officially and legally a meeting of the Department of Ophthalmology quality-review committee--Waring, Travis Meredith, and Doyle Stulting. The others present—Louis Wilson, Hank Kaplan, and Bill Coles—were guests; David Campbell was speaking in Washington, D.C. The meeting's results were to be confidential and were peer protected.

The term "peer protection" refers to the legal rights afforded an official hospital or university review committee. In order to encourage open dialogue about sensitive matters, state legislatures passed laws that prevented the contents of such meetings from being used by lawyers pursuing malpractice lawsuits.

Waring reviewed the activities of the committee and listed the questionable activities of Cavanagh. He proposed a format for the committee to discuss each issue individually and vote its conclusions. They would decide later what to do with their conclusions, but a report of some kind would be necessary. It was 7:00, time for Doyle Stulting to read the first topic. Stulting had been appointed the secretary and note-taker. His notes constituted the minutes for this meeting and all subsequent ones. These notes, David Campbell's dictated recollections, and the transcript of a taped meeting by Allen

Gammon provide the documentation for my description of the following series of meetings.

Stulting began with the first issue on the list, the surgery on Sargus Houston and specifically the charges of chart alterations and cover-up. There was no question that changes in the charts were made. Phil Newman acknowledged some of them because he made them, unmade them, and put his initials by his changes.

But somebody else crossed out "OD," not correctly crossing it out with a line through it, but totally obliterating it, and put "OS." This change was made only in Cavanagh's clinic chart, not in the hospital chart or the copy that went to pathology. Also, the hospital chart had some additions made to it including, "cat OS, rough surface, and consider canthoplasty." This notation was not in the clinic chart or the pathology chart.

The discussion was summarized by Dr. Stulting:

Discussion centered around the alteration to the original outpatient chart (OD to OS). It was pointed out that the handwriting was not consistent with HDC's.

J. Switz and P Newman were considered as author of the change. Motives for the change were unclear.

Kaplan moved the following: "One, the chart was altered. Two, we have no evidence that Dwight was the author of these changes."

Bill Coles seconded the motion.

Stulting recorded the vote as 5–0 in favor.

Stulting introduced the next issue, extra billing by Cavanagh. In certain transplants, Cavanagh had submitted an extra charge for removal of a retrocorneal fibrous membrane (RCFM). He did this for many patients with keratoconus, but there is no such membrane in that disease. And, as would be expected, pathology reported no membrane on the specimens.

He moved the following: "The data suggests that patients were billed for excision of RCFM. We cannot determine whether the data presented represents purposeful billing for surgery not performed."

Meredith seconded, and the vote was 5–0.

Stulting moved to the third topic, separate billing for intraocular and extraocular procedures. Years later, the FBI investigated Cavanagh's unique system of billing for his cases. (Author's note: No official action from the FBI was ever taken.)

Cavanagh, when dictating his operative notes and submitting bills, had devised his own methods and set of rules. Medicare and insurance regulations require that, if several procedures are done on a patient, one operative note is to be dictated and one bill submitted. The most expensive procedure—for example, corneal transplant—is paid at full charges, while the other procedures—such as cataract surgery, lens implantation, and lid surgery—are paid at less than the full rate. Cavanagh substituted his own policy. If he did several procedures inside the eye, these were dictated in one note. But if he also did a lid procedure, he dictated a separate note and thus generated a full fee for this added work. He felt this was justified since he was operating on separate tissue. After dictation, he would carefully write the charge for each procedure on a separate slip. He persisted in the practice of separate operative notes, even though no one else in his department followed suit and a few had questioned the practice as illegal.

The discussion of this issue concluded, Doyle Stulting offered a motion. He moved that the operative procedures were performed and that billing practices for various procedures vary among department members. Further, that no compromises of patient care or inappropriate billing occurred. After Meredith's second, all voted in favor.

Waring presented the next issue, doing transplants for Fuchs' dystrophy when the pathology turned out to be normal. He had looked at the slides with John Wright and reviewed over 150 charts from 1983 to 1984. They found thirty "normal" corneas, and Dr. Waring had reviewed nineteen charts in detail, finding five "questionable" charts. After discussion, Dr. Meredith offered the motion that was approved: In these five cases, clinical and pathological findings apparently failed to support the clinical diagnosis to justify penetrating keratoplasty.

The next issue was alterations in the charts. The fellows and techs had complained about this for years. Waring and Stulting's review had focused on acuity changes. Cavanagh would just strike out whatever the fellow or tech put, and he would insert a worse vision. They had not discovered a single chart in which he inserted a better vision, at least preoperatively.

After a long discussion, Dr. Hank Kaplan moved that "visual acuities were consistently altered in a pattern that led to surgery in the charts presented; however, [they did] not have sufficient information to conclude that there has been inappropriate surgery performed."

The next issue was derogatory letters written by Cavanagh, the most inflammatory being one defaming a colleague at the Medical College of Georgia. Kaplan dispatched with this by moving that the contents had no bearing on patient care.

Waring took up the final issue, undiagnosed glaucoma, and presented seven cases he had culled from Cavanagh's patients.

The group picked apart the seven charts, rejecting the claim of neglected glaucoma except in one. Stulting moved that "The summary provided by Dr. David Campbell [indicated] inadequate management of increased pressure." Meredith seconded, and it passed.

Waring quickly stood as the group was packing up their papers. It was 1:00 in the morning. He reminded the troops of another meeting in two days. No one was to talk to anyone.

THURSDAY, OCTOBER 4, 1984
EMORY DENTAL SCHOOL

George Waring called to order the second meeting of the expanded quality-review committee and welcomed two new guests, Dr. David Campbell and Felton Jenkins, an attorney from the well known firm of King & Spalding. Jenkins had been advising Waring for a year on the formation and conduct of the committee. For Campbell's benefit, Waring repeated the charge of the committee, the fact that the four senior, tenured faculty—Campbell, Wilson, Coles, and Kaplan—were guests and the need for confidentiality. Campbell surveyed the room and found little comfort. He was alone.

Jenkins stayed for three hours as the group argued the issues back and forth. Jenkins noted that the group should not act in any legal sense unless it could prove unequivocal wrongdoing on Cavanagh's part. If it could, then money should be repaid, possibly to all patients who had been illegally charged, including Houston.

As the meeting dragged on, David Campbell watched in amazement as Dr. Kaplan refuted every negative statement about Cavanagh. Travis Meredith ran a close second in vociferous opposition to any conclusion or vote that would incriminate the chairman.

But it wasn't just Kaplan and Meredith. Lou Wilson took Waring aback when he asked who saw Waring's patients when Waring was out of town, which frequently happened.

Waring's fellow did, who else? And the fellow made the medical decisions. And then Emory billed insurance companies in Waring's name.

Did Waring know that was illegal? Medicare didn't allow that. Wilson went on, wondering if anyone in the room had a clue what Emory would do with their new building if the department blew up. Instead of an eye center, Emory would have a nice dog lab for the medical students.

Travis Meredith asked David Campbell if Campbell's fellow was still doing lasers even though Meredith had told him a while ago he wasn't licensed.

On and on, Lou Wilson asked if any of those present could withstand a Medicare investigation, and Campbell remembers thinking that no court of law would convict Cavanagh based on that night's wrangling. If the attorney wanted unequivocal proof of legal wrongdoing before the department could take legal action, it wasn't there in this group.

After three hours, Waring called for a vote on the issue of interviewing Dwight Cavanagh at the next meeting, scheduled for the next evening. Stulting's notes on the Felton discussion were later blanked out, but the remaining notes show that the group voted unanimously to interview Cavanagh and spent the next few minutes assigning topics for each to present to him. Campbell would present the neglected glaucoma patients.

Friday, October 5, 1984
Emory Dental School

Dr. Waring addressed Dwight Cavanagh as the rest of the official committee and tenured faculty listened soberly. Waring briefly reviewed the history of the committee, pointing out that the task of investigating their chairman was not an easy one. Nevertheless, they had wrestled with very serious allegations and felt it only fair to get Cavanagh's responses to the issues.

After two hours, Cavanagh left, and Waring called the committee to order after a break. At this point, Stulting's notes begin, as he did not record Cavanagh's responses or the discussion. Despite the fact that it was 7:00 on a Friday night, Waring wanted to push ahead and review the votes and conclusions of the first meeting, now that David Campbell was present and they had heard Cavanagh's version of the issues.

So it began. Doyle Stulting led off with chart alterations. Cavanagh had just denied making any of these changes, and the group, sans Campbell three nights ago, had voted that they had no evidence to incriminate Cavanagh. David Campbell, sitting across the table from Meredith and Kaplan, wondered who else would have made them. And had anyone talked to Phil Newman or Genevieve Switz to get their input?

Now the challenge was out in the open, and the room erupted. Campbell, the lone dissenter, had dared to challenge the vote of the previous night. After all, if Phil Newman had owned up to his chart alterations, and if there were several others in different handwriting, who besides Cavanagh would be motivated to make the changes? Who else would have the opportunity? So the debate raged until a new vote was ordered.

On this vote, the committee split the motion. All agreed that the chart had been altered. Six voted that the handwriting did not appear to be Cavanagh's. Dr. Campbell dissented and voted against the motion, as he felt the handwriting was Cavanagh's.

The next issue was just as contentious—membrane removal billed for eyes that had no membrane to be removed. Dr. Cavanagh had explained that he used the code for removal of retrocorneal membrane when he took the extra time to bevel a wound. He claimed he didn't know what the charges were or what went through to the billing office or the insurance company. He knew there was no membrane in keratoconus, but he felt he should be able to bill extra when he beveled the wound and did some extra work.

The club and a few of the others felt Cavanagh's explanation was sufficient. They wanted to leave this one as they had voted two nights previously ("We cannot determine whether the data presented represents purposeful billing for surgery not performed").

Campbell would have none of it. They had all seen Cavanagh hunched over the billing slips, giving precise instructions to the business office about the charges for each patient. Waring had verified that Cavanagh's instructions were regarded as law by the billing office. Cavanagh's defense didn't hold up, at least not to David Campbell.

Back and forth went the argument, until someone made this motion: "In the case of membranectomy, there is no conclusive evidence that Dr. Cavanagh intentionally misrepresented the procedure performed for personal gain.... We feel this terminology has been misleading and support his discontinuation of the use of imprecise terminology for op reports for keratoconus." The group voted in favor, 6–1, Campbell the lone dissenter.

Doyle Stulting moved them through the misdiagnosed Fuchs' dystrophy patients. Earlier in that evening, Cavanagh had admitted an error in judgment on Mattie Brown, that she did not have Fuchs'. The other cases reviewed by George Waring were clear-cut. The group strengthened the motion of two nights ago by voting unanimously that "The indications for surgery in these cases reviewed were not supported by clinical and histopathological data available."

Waring asked Campbell to discuss the neglected glaucoma patients. In yet another challenge to the group, Campbell said he couldn't believe they had thrown out all of the charts but one on Tuesday night. Dr. Allen had left the faculty because of this issue. Cavanagh had confessed earlier that evening that these patients "slipped through the cracks." He had admitted his guilt. If Cavanagh himself couldn't defend these cases, and the six charts presented to the group were a small portion of the total, how could this group absolve the chief of neglect?

Still there was argument, but finally the following passed 6–0: "We conclude that this visual loss occurred because of an overburdened medical practice, and the patients did not receive optimum medical care."

It was late, their Friday evening was ruined, and there was more to come. Dr. Stulting presented the chart falsifications, and Dr. Kaplan rose to Cavanagh's defense. Cavanagh had just admitted that he had stopped doing this almost a year ago. He had measured the vision in a bright room, not a dark room, and they all knew that bright light intensifies glare and reduces vision, so what was the problem? In Kaplan's view, the different visual acuities recorded by Cavanagh were justified by the different lighting conditions.

Travis Meredith demurred; chart falsification had bothered him more than all the other issues. So many charts....

Campbell observed that if Cavanagh's method of checking vision was medically sound, why did he stop that method a year ago?

The group was too fatigued to continue arguing. A new motion was supported by everyone: "The alterations in visual acuity were made in a direction to justify surgery, and in some of these cases the changes may have resulted in inappropriately early surgery."

After a brief discussion of the last issue—the derogatory letters, letters that Cavanagh had acknowledged were inappropriate—the group made no change from the vote of several days ago: no harm done to patients. Everyone stood, then stretched, grabbed papers, glared at their watches, and began five different conversations.

Waring shouted over the din that they weren't through. They had a meeting Monday night, where David Campbell was to bring opinions from two other lawyers, and they had to decide what to do with the report.

* * *

As the enormity and potential ramifications of the committee work became clear to David Campbell, he began to document the events. He knew that Allen Gammon had already begun secretly taping all his conversations and meetings, but Campbell couldn't go that far. He did begin taping his recollections within a few days of a meeting, planning for later transcription.

His first tape began:

I have just lived through two of the toughest days of my life with a sense of extreme disappointment after the first meeting [Thursday, October 4].... *Thursday night, it became apparent, however, that of the seven faculty members, there were...strong supporters of Dwight, there were strong supporters of the opinion that this investigation should not go beyond the Department of Ophthalmology. The strongest supporter of Dwight was Henry Kaplan. He simply would not hear of any negative remarks and always refuted them.... Travis Meredith also felt strongly about this, and what their reasons are right now, I can only conjecture. I feel that they both feel that if there is some kind of reshuffling in the department, and if Dwight loses his job, that they will both be big losers. Why, I don't know. Henry may feel that his endowed chair would be in jeopardy and his high position in the department as director of research. Travis may feel his financial return may be in jeopardy. It may be that Dwight is helping Travis in ways that are unknown, and he would also lose his number-two position in the department. Travis and Dwight both went to Hopkins. There may be a fraternal tie there that would be understandable....*

I'm now on the Georgia back road where I spent many hours this spring working out all of my emotional reaction to this terrible affair and slowly coming to the conclusion that somehow, even if it destroys me, I cannot condone it, I cannot live with it, I cannot allow it to go on in any way. Dwight accepted rather easily the wrongdoing in regard to his glaucoma patients, and I was surprised at that.... We are approaching a position where Dwight is about to become that powerful [referring to Cavanagh becoming a nationally known ophthalmologist], *and he is clearly unethical and amoral, and if he is allowed to become this powerful, so that he can do anything, and he takes his amoral behavior into the area of all of ophthalmology, then not only the department at Emory will be hurt, but ophthalmology and medicine in general will be hurt.*

* * *

David Campbell's dictated notes of October 10 reflect his activities of the previous three days:

October 10, 1984. Had dinner with the Warings and spent a good part of Sunday night [October 7] *until about 10:00 reviewing all of the records and all of the minutes of the meetings.*

Monday, I had a morning appointment with Harry Pritchett [Campbell's minister]; *talked with him about forty-five minutes, and fascinatingly he just said to me that he couldn't help me but that he would put his arm around my shoulder. And, he quoted Luther to me: "Here I stand. I can do no other. God help me." And, he said that maybe I had come in my life to that point, and, in a way, I had.*

I then on Sunday had had about a forty-five-minute conversation with Bill Ragsdale [Campbell's attorney] after church, and on Monday at 3:00 I had a one-hour conversation with Bill and Penn Spell, his partner in litigation. And Penn brought up more questions than he answered...what the rules are of the American Academy of Ophthalmology..., what the insurance coverage was and what our obligations were there... i.e., if we know of some potential liability and we don't bring it to the attention of the carrier, are we then uninsured?

And of course, then there's the federal government, Medicare, Medicaid fraud, which really gets into a serious area of litigation. This is potentially so serious that it would probably be best to pay the money back now, rather than to have them find out that we know about this, that we are hanging on to the money, and have them come after us for it.

MONDAY, OCTOBER 8, 1984
EMORY DENTAL SCHOOL

The Friday-night group convened at 6:25 PM. For the committee, it was the fourth night devoted to the Cavanagh review. Stulting's notes reflect that, as usual, Waring called the group to order, and he then called on David Campbell to review the opinions of the two attorneys he had consulted.

Both lawyers had agreed that it was unprecedented for a faculty to investigate its chairman and raised the question of whether this group could render an unbiased opinion about Dr. Cavanagh.

Again, Campbell was interrupted by Wilson, Meredith, or Kaplan. They questioned Campbell's motives, worried about his lawyers, and resented his lack of loyalty. The attorneys had advised that a report be sent to Emory's administration, and the fight began.

David Campbell watched in amazement as the debate raged. After an hour of fighting about the report and its implications, the group approved a statement to introduce its specific findings and conclusions: "The committee reviewed a number of documents relating to medical care and found this standard of care was on occasion inappropriate for this department. Specific areas of concern include inaccuracies in dictated operative notes, inappropriate chart documentation of surgical indications, discrepancies between clinical and pathological diagnoses, and inadequate management in some cases of glaucoma."

Campbell then moved that Cavanagh reduce his practice load and that all his surgical cases be reviewed. It passed and was limited to six months by Stulting's motion.

By this point, the room was littered with empty Coke cans and sandwich wrappers, and everybody wanted to go home. Bill Coles then moved that they send their report to Charles Hatcher.

The room exploded again as Kaplan shouted, "No, no, no." He totally opposed that idea. They were a review committee for the eye department and not in Hatcher's chain of command. He argued that their findings should stay there, within the department. Others spoke up, wanting it to go to Emory's Ethics Committee.

Campbell watched the motion go down in defeat, 4–3. He dictated two days later: *I can remember that I just almost probably slumped back in my chair, and I thought to myself, "Holy shit! This whole thing is back on my shoulders alone. Mine and Allen's. But, for now, mine." Well, slumped in my chair with my reaction, then the most incredible conversion occurred within the room. Something had happened which the majority, given the reality, felt very uncomfortable with, and people started to talk about this and that, I don't remember exactly what. What I do remember was that Lou Wilson looked straight across the table at me and said, "Alright, David Campbell, now that we have voted this way, what are you going to do? Are you going to take this up* [to a higher level at Emory]*?" And I said, "Gentlemen, I don't know what I'm going to do. I have not thought it all out."*

The group then speculated whether Allen Gammon might take the report to a higher level and eventually decided to send a report to Charles Hatcher. The group specifically excluded George Waring from the meeting with Hatcher; only Travis Meredith and Lou Wilson were to present the findings.

Campbell recollects: *So a new motion was made that we take the rather bland summary, and I don't remember whether we ever decided whether we would take a copy of the minutes along or not, but take a rather bland summary up to Charlie Hatcher. At this point, I was weak, and I was feeling that I could not push hard on this group, so I didn't press. But there was a revote, and Travis* [Meredith] *changed his vote, and Lou* [Wilson] *changed his vote. Henry* [Kaplan] *abstained, giving a strong indication of exactly where Henry was coming from.... And George* [Waring] *did not have to vote, so George never had to commit himself, never had to show himself against Dwight the whole damn time....*

If Charlie [Hatcher], *and this is my only hope, if Charlie were to read the minutes, a responsible person, I do not think, could read those minutes without wanting to know more about it, without realizing he had to form an impartial committee to come to some answers about it.*

If, however, one wanted a mere cover-up, then that would be it, and from what people have told me, I think that is probably the case.... In other words, Travis clearly gave me the opinion that this was not going to bother Charlie very much.

[Meredith had reported to Campbell that they had presented the report to Hatcher, and neither Meredith nor Wilson could get a read on Hatcher's reaction.]

So there I was on Tuesday left with the shattering realization that after all of this work, we were still going to get, in effect, a non-response, a cover-up. But some very good things have happened. The damage to patients has been stopped. That was the most important thing, and it has stopped. And a second very good thing has happened, and that is that the knowledge about this has gone to the appropriate authority, and therefore, that we as members in the Department of Ophthalmology are, and should be, absolved of any further obligations, and that if anything of a serious nature comes up, we cannot be held personally responsible.

* * *

During the week between meetings, Allen Gammon asked Dr. Waring for permission to look at all the minutes, and Waring agreed. Some of the faculty, afraid of Gammon, criticized Waring for allowing Gammon access to the minutes, patients' names and all. Waring countered that they had all voted to share this material with the junior faculty at the next meeting, and he doubted there was any harm in letting Gammon have it a few days early.

* * *

MONDAY, OCTOBER 15, 1984
EMORY DENTAL SCHOOL

Eleven ophthalmology faculty members, all with tenure or on track for tenure, met on this night. The new attendees were Ms. Frankie Stegall, head orthoptist, and Drs. Robert Spector, Alan Kozarsky, Allen Gammon, and John Wright.

David Campbell looked around the room, happy and relieved to see allies. He was not alone for this meeting. Allen Gammon, of course, was his main support. Not only was Gammon present, but unbeknownst to the rest, his tape recorder was running. But John Wright had agonized over the pathology; Alan Kozarsky had warned about problems after a few weeks on Cavanagh's service. They were here and certainly would speak up, wouldn't they? Campbell settled back as George Waring took over.

The transcripts of Gammon's tapes show that Waring opened with a review of the events of the previous week. He reported that

Wilson and Meredith had met with Hatcher and that the Waring committee had made three recommendations:

1. Cavanagh greatly curtail his practice.
2. Cavanagh's preoperative charts be monitored for six months.
3. Cavanagh's office charts be monitored monthly.

Of Dr. Hatcher's reaction to the meeting with Wilson and Meredith, Dr. Wilson said, "Charles doesn't react. It's like talking to the great Buddha. You just simply talk to the man, and he listens."

Now, Waring wanted to go through these issues one-by-one with all the faculty. Tonight was the night to get things out, discussed, and resolved.

First, the Houston chart and the alterations. The committee had concluded that the chart had been changed; that was obvious. But they couldn't be sure Dwight did it, so they said that in the report.

Waring barely had the words out before the questions hammered him. What do they mean, they couldn't be sure? Who else would do it or even have a chance to do it, since Dwight had the chart? Dwight was the attending physician. Wasn't he responsible for the chart? Did he know about these changes?

Travis Meredith jumped in to defend his chief. They had to work with facts and facts alone. No one knew for sure that Cavanagh had made the other chart changes.

Taken aback, the group fell silent except for Gammon. What did Phil Newman say? Or Genevieve Switz? They were there.

Travis Meredith: "It would not make any difference if Phil Newman came in now and gave a different story to us.... It would not change my mind at all if the man comes in and says it is his opinion that Dwight changed it and he had no direct evidence."

David Campbell heard the challenges posed by the new attendees with joy. He was not fighting this battle by himself tonight. Campbell spoke up here and there to clarify his position and his previous vote.

He couldn't be sure the handwriting wasn't Cavanagh's and wasn't going to be bullied about it.

The discussion died down, and Waring went on to the billing irregularities.

The crowd treated the second issue just as rudely. Widespread hoots greeted the conclusion that, in regard to billing for retrocorneal membranes, Cavanagh did not "intentionally misrepresent the procedure for financial gain."

Question: "How many times was it done?"

Waring: "Oh, it would be a few hundred."

Comment: "The other thing that I found difficult to swallow was this, was the whole idea of...calling this a retrocorneal fibrous membrane. I mean the terminology is not even close to trimming or beveling or modifying that to fit.

"And if you read the operative note, the operative note talked about stripping tissue from the angle and things like this, which are light years from beveling the wound so you get a better fit.

"And the other thing, the claim for confusion because of a heavy load doesn't hold water as far as I'm concerned because the pattern is so consistent. That's not confusion."

This meeting was not intended for revoting the issues, and after the discussion of billing died, Waring moved to the issue of derogatory letters. The committee had dismissed this issue because it hadn't affected patient care. But, Dr. Waring noted, Cavanagh had potentially embarrassed the entire university with critical statements he had made about other doctors in the state. When the committee had shown Cavanagh the letter he wrote about the Augusta doctor, he admitted that he had made a mistake.

Further, Waring pointed out the occasions when Cavanagh had criticized them, his own faculty. Here's what he said a few years ago about Waring: "Young Dr. Waring has joined our faculty, and he's just learning how to take care of these things. I'll manage with so-and-so for you, and I'm sure that as his skills improve, he will become an improved physician." After Waring had confronted his chairman, Cavanagh had quit making such comments.

Dr. Gammon jumped in. Cavanagh had told him not to refer his problem patients to certain Emory ophthalmologists.

Waring added that Cavanagh had criticized many of them to him behind their backs. And he had heard that Cavanagh had spoken behind Waring's back to some of the doctors present in the room. This was terrible. It was manipulative, divisive, and made the faculty distrust each other. Cavanagh had further admitted he had an "acid tongue" but would try to do better. At any rate, it was in the report, and Cavanagh knew about the issue.

Finally the meeting approached an end. Waring summarized the recommendations curtailing Cavanagh's practice and monitoring the charts. True, Cavanagh's letter of a few weeks ago had announced he was cutting back on his clinical activities, but the committee wanted to go on record with its own set of recommendations. Henceforth, Cavanagh was to do only two cases per week, see only a few office patients, and spend the majority of his time on administration and research. George Waring concluded that he didn't see how a faculty committee could do any more to its chairman. They'd cut him back, reported the problem areas, and communicated with the vice president of Health Affairs. If anything else was to happen, higher authorities than them would have to act.

David Campbell went straight home, talked with his wife for a while, and began dictating:

I got out of the rat race and took a long, pleasurable weekend in Asheville, North Carolina...and it was a pleasure to leave the agony of the day-to-day living at the Emory Clinic.... I had talked with Frank Bell [former retina faculty and Musketeer] *one evening prior, and he told me something that encouraged me, and that was that he knew what was going on, and that I had his support. He said that many of the other ophthalmologists in Atlanta, and indeed around the state of Georgia, knew what was going on; they knew about the wrong-eye case, they knew about the alterations in the charts, and they knew about the early and unwarranted surgery. They were waiting to see what Emory would do about it.*

Back Sunday night to an incredibly lousy feeling that I was back at Emory, that I was back at the cesspool and that the train which I thought was going to roll inevitably downhill toward truth and freedom and free air had come to a stop and was halted. I went through my work today in a deep depression, and it was not with any great enthusiasm that I attended the faculty meeting tonight at 6:00.

Travis and Henry and Lou were joking and yukking it up as they have in front of other meetings, which I guess has always led me to feel that, one, they must feel that they've got either the meeting in the bag or, two, that they want to give the impression that these issues are of such a light-hearted nature that free joking is a part of a meeting dealing with matters of such real concern.

But now there were other faculty members there tonight. I didn't sit alone around that table. There were twelve instead of six.

A very dramatic announcement was made about halfway through the meeting that Dwight had gone to see a lawyer about all of this, that he'd gone to see Hunter Allen, and that Hunter had then called Travis to tell him to be very careful about not saying anything that could be regarded as slander, and that he had then called George Waring, and George said it had been a very abrupt and nasty phone call...

Bob Spector spoke very strongly from time to time about the fact that there seemed to be real wrongs here.... Allen [Gammon] kept hammering the point home over and over that we did not know the truth of this matter, that we did not know all that we needed to know about it, that two people involved had not been questioned.

The final incident that I forgot to record was the incredible table-slamming episode by Travis. We were talking about covering our liabilities and being certain that we had told Charlie [Hatcher] all that he needed to know, and I stated that we did not know, i.e., the rest of us, what Charlie had been told, and at that point Travis took that to mean that I was implying that he was a liar or that

I was impugning his honesty, and he started slamming the table, and I believe he slammed it about three of four times, harder and harder each time, to the point where he almost broke the table. I told him that I did not intend to in any way impugn his honesty, and he apologized rather quickly.

I finished the dictation [of the Monday faculty meeting] *about 1:30 in the morning. Nawrie* [his wife] *and I talked for a while. We even talked about transferring the house to her name* [in case of future legal action against the department or Campbell individually. The Clinic was a legal partnership, meaning that each partner could be held liable for the misdeeds of another partner]. *She asked me if I could live with Dwight Cavanagh personally at this point, and my answer to that is I think I can, if he treats me fairly and, as I said, if I see a conversion to honesty in his dealings.... But I don't care to be vindictive, and I think that at this point if we were to carry it further, that a lot more would crash, that Emory's reputation would crash, the reputation of the clinic, etc.*

My job for the rest of the day, then, and over the next two days, is to try and get that message across to people and at this point to try and slow down the gears that are inexorably moving toward total destruction. One of the questions that comes up, of course, was someone in the faculty informing Dwight of the committee delibera-tions at every point, and, of course, did this have something to do with the fact that Dwight "voluntarily" decided to cut back.

CHAPTER SIX

LAWSUIT

OCTOBER 1984

Memo

TO: Dr. David G. Campbell
FROM: H. Dwight Cavanagh, M.D.
DATE: October 18, 1984
RE: Status of Promotion to Full Professor

I have today received, correlated, and signed all neces-sary paperwork for your promotion to Professor and have sent same to the Dean.

I have no doubt that the request will be acted upon posi-tively.

It takes about three to four weeks to clear the Council of Chairmen; and thus, very likely, can be announced at the Academy meeting.

I thought you would like to know this.

HDC/po

* * *

OCTOBER 20, 1984

Dorothy Fuller, Sargus Houston's niece, who lived in Decatur, Georgia, hung up the phone, puzzled, and turned to her husband, Levi. Someone named Pat Haverty wanted to come by to tell them something about Uncle Sargus. Had Levi ever heard that name?

The man who called himself Pat Haverty came to the Fullers' house on Sunday, October 21, and told Sargus Houston's niece that Dr. Cavanagh made a mistake when he operated on Houston's eye. He was supposed to do the right eye, but he got mixed up, and he operated on that left eye by mistake. That was his good eye. It didn't need surgery. Did the family know about that?

No, they didn't. They never knew. They thought the doctor knew best.

Well, their uncle was wronged, lied to. How well could he see?

She felt he saw poorly, but Houston would say he saw just fine.

Haverty came to the real reason for his visit: The family needed to see a lawyer. They had a case. No doctor should be able to get away with what that Dr. Cavanagh did—an operation on somebody's wrong eye—and not own up to it. Haverty had a list of names, all good lawyers, not afraid to take on a doctor, even if he was at Emory.

Fuller took the names, said good-bye to the man, and never saw him again. She needed to talk to the family. She could not make this decision by herself. She and Levi looked over the list of names. The name at the top was Taylor W. Jones.

* * *

The department moved into the new eye center in November. Lou Wilson moved back out to the center from his office in downtown Atlanta and began monitoring Cavanagh's charts. Campbell and the glaucoma section settled into the third floor, and the cornea section settled into the fourth floor. No longer was the faculty crowded cheek-to-jowl. Their own operating room was downstairs, and patients loved the new atmosphere.

Since 1978 the eye department had grown from a three–M.D. faculty to an eighteen–M.D. faculty. During that time, the number of basic science researchers and PhDs had increased from two to twelve, residents from twelve to fifteen, and fellows from nine to sixteen. Grants totaled $2,000,000 as opposed to $50,000 in 1976. Cavanagh had indeed done what no one before him had: he had built the eye center and dramatically grown the department.

Those of us practicing in town viewed Emory's growth with mixed feelings. Every new faculty member represented another subspecialist looking for patients, so competition increased. Yet this was competition more in theory than fact. Atlanta continued to grow, adding thousands of new citizens each year, and none of us lacked for patients. High-quality colleagues at Emory were a resource for help with problem patients, and the conferences provided valuable teaching. On balance, the growth in the eye department was positive from the perspective of private practitioners, at least in my view. Atlanta needed a strong Emory, and we had a valuable presence in an enhanced eye department.

* * *

December 1984

George Waring, delayed by the move into the eye center, officially terminated his committee's duty by sending a letter to Hatcher, the eye faculty, and Cavanagh. He quoted the findings of the committee, ending his letter to Hatcher with the following:

The Medical Care Review Committee has terminated its retrospective review of some aspects of the practice of ophthalmology by H. Dwight Cavanagh, M.D. The findings have been discussed both with Dr. Cavanagh and the tenure-track faculty. The documents examined and the minutes of the meetings are enclosed.

We ask that you formally discharge us from further responsibility in pursuit of this matter and that unresolved issues be handled as you feel appropriate.

Dr. Waring had punted the issue up the chain as his committee and he had wanted. They had done all they could, and it was time for administration to act. Charles Hatcher responded by sending the report to Dr. Garland Perdue.

By this time, Garland Perdue was director of the Emory Clinic, its CEO, as well as medical director of Emory University Hospital. The Emory physicians liked Perdue.

Perdue discussed Waring's report with three ophthalmologists—Wilson, Kaplan, and Meredith—as well as two other department chairs at Emory. Aside from writing an official letter to Wilson requesting monthly reports on the monitoring of Cavanagh's practice, Perdue did nothing. The rest of the administration followed suit.

Emory's administration acted as though the matter was settled. But the eye department was different; it seethed, and the move to the center provided no balm.

An anguished letter from George Waring to Cavanagh gives light to the department's unease.

DECEMBER 14, 1984

Dear Dwight,

The circumstances of the past few months have strained our relationship. My conversation with Lynne [Cavanagh's wife] at the Emory alumni academy party and with you on December 6 led me to explain the background and the reasoning that resulted in the quality-care review of your practice. My purpose is to be sure that you understand that I instigated no witch hunt or investigation, that the situation arose from concerns of many members of our department over a number of years, and that I worked hard to bring a constructive solution to a difficult and dangerous problem....

When I came to Emory in 1979, it became apparent that the style of medical practice differed markedly among the faculty. For about three years, whenever one of the residents, fellows, or other faculty members would make observations about these differences, I would give the stock answer, "One of the advantages of being at Emory is that we have a diverse faculty with different approaches to ophthalmic problems; this is part of the richness of our department." In late 1982, however, the atmosphere began to change. Residents and fellows raised more pointed questions about the decisions you made in patient care, but I persisted in the stock answer....

By 1983 this questioning changed to concern and even accusations from an increasing number of faculty, residents, fellows, and technical staff. I believe some faculty spoke to you personally about the quality of care in specific situations during this time. I remained a distant observer....

During the first nine months of 1984, an increasing number of accusations concerning your practice were made by faculty and staff, both among themselves and to me. These included:

1. *Alterations of visual acuity on the chart*
2. *Surgery on eyes for diseases that did not exist*
3. *Inappropriate early surgery for minimal disease*
4. *Multiple billings for procedures performed at the same operation*
5. *Fraudulent billing for surgical procedures not performed*
6. *Inappropriate management of patients leading to severe loss of vision.*

These accusations came so frequently from many different individuals it was no longer possible to account for them by appeal to different practice styles.... This was a groundswell of concern and fear that resulted in extremely severe accusations.... A spirit of fear and personal liability spread among us. Questions of lawsuits and concerns about occupancy of the eye center arose....

Dr. Waring spent another page of tightly spaced paragraphs reviewing the history of the recent committee meetings and then explained why he did not speak with Cavanagh personally before the committee met:

The first reason is that I did not think you would listen to me. You may remember when we chatted at the Kansas City Club in 1978, as I was trying to decide whether to join the faculty here, I suggested that you and I would have one major problem: I did not think you would listen to me. I believe this has been true on many other occasions, Dwight, the most sensitive being when I took the time to write you a seven-page handwritten letter in July 1983 on a very personal and professional relationship, and you never responded in any way whatsoever. Many others in our department think you do not hear what people are saying to you, rather what you want to hear.

The second reason I did not sit down with you was that the accusations were extremely serious. It seemed most inappropriate for me to wander into your office and say "You know what they're saying about you" on the basis of no review of the evidence....

The third reason I did not speak with you is that I was afraid. I was afraid not only of the seriousness of the accusations and the problems that had surfaced, but also that you might become angry and retaliate against me by withdrawing support and undermining my efforts both at Emory and extramurally. You have a reputation of dividing people into favored and un-favored categories, and I feared becoming "un-favored."

The fourth reason I did not come to talk to you was that others in the department had told me that they had sat down and reviewed these questions with you, and that it seemed to have little effect on your practice.

I emphasize to you that I am in no way responsible for the opinions or the behavior of my faculty colleagues. Those who chose to speak to others outside the department and to seek legal counsel outside the department did so on their own....

In 1979, some of our colleagues said you and I could never work at peace in the same department. Let's prove them wrong. I look forward to discussing this with you further.

Sincerely,
George

* * *

JANUARY **1985**

David Campbell resumed dictating his activities this month: *January 10, 1985.... The Cavanagh affair just will not go away. It appears that, both before my discussion with Dwight and after, he has been coming after me now in regard to the visual-fields service.* [The measurement of the extent of peripheral vision, the "visual field," is integral to the evaluation of a glaucoma patient. Cavanagh was proposing to give control of the technicians who performed this evaluation to Dr. Robert Spector, a neuro-ophthalmologist who also heavily utilized visual-field examination. The result would have been loss of income to Campbell and reduced control over the scheduling of his patients.]

I had a discussion this morning with Bob Spector and asked him if he had had a discussion with Dwight, and he said that he had, and he said that Dwight had asked him to run the visual-fields service. And I told him that that would be unacceptable....

Bill Coles and I had dinner from quarter to 7:00 to 10:00. When Bill Coles came [to Emory to head up residency teaching and the Grady program], *he was told that he would be mainly administrating, which he did, and he was proud of the job he had done down at Grady, and he felt that he had done a better job than anyone else had done. He mentioned Dwight* [who, as department chairman, was nominally head of Grady] *had never been down there. He said that when the financial crunch came, all of a sudden he was told he had to generate his income, then he had secretaries removed, then he was down to half a secretary, and he said he had to pay his secretary out of his own pocket for eight months. He described frequent frustrations with Dwight and agrees that Dwight is a horrible internal administrator and agrees that Dwight's main tactic is to do something that harms a person and to not tell the person that he has done it. Gutter politics. You not only do something that harms a person, but you don't tell that person about it, in a scheming fashion, so that that person finds out that he has had a knife placed in his back, not from Dwight who has done it, but from someone else....*

Dwight may be coming after me now to show the administration that he had to do harmful things against me and, therefore, that if I do something against him my reason was not concern for patients, etc., but my reason was to get back at Dwight. Dwight seems to feel he can overcome this, and this seems to be his tactic.

So I go home to thrust it all into the file and to totally forget about it for a good long while. To put every thought out of my mind for at least three weeks and then perhaps reassess the whole situation. If Dwight's tactic is to put a person into such turmoil that he can get no work done, and I have told him that I am in that state, then he has won, just as he has beaten Allen. And I show great strength by not allowing this to happen…. I think the only way I can find inner peace, though, is to forgive Dwight, and that I must do now.

* * *

LATE JANUARY 1985

The family told their uncle, Sargus, that it was time to go. He needed his coat; it was cold. They guided him into the back of the car and placed his hands on the door and seat so he could find his way. Sargus Houston was in the car heading from Macon to Atlanta, but this trip was different. The destination was downtown Atlanta, not Emory. He and his family had an appointment with Taylor Jones, an attorney on the list given to Dorothy Fuller three months earlier. Houston's next scheduled appointment with Dr. Cavanagh was not until February.

Taylor Jones and Dwight Cavanagh had tangled before. In the early 1980s, Cavanagh had fired a resident for incompetence. Jones had represented the resident and won reinstatement for him.

Jones, a litigator who represented plaintiffs in malpractice suits against doctors, heard Houston's story with growing incredulity and anger. He had never heard a story quite like this one. Operating on the wrong side is rare; concealing the truth is even rarer. Jones knew that the legal charge for operating on the wrong site involved more than just malpractice. Since Houston had not given permission for Cavanagh to operate on the left eye at all, Jones could charge the surgeon with battery in addition.

Before leaving, Houston signed a boilerplate agreement entitled "Contract for Employment—Authority to Represent." Houston would pay no retainer and agreed that he would pay his attorneys, from the proceeds of the recovery, the following fee:

33 1/3% If settled without filing suit;

40% In the event a suit is filed;
50% If a motion for new trial, or an appeal is taken from the
lower court by either side, or if garnishment or any proceed-
ing after judgment has to be brought to collect the judgment
or any portion thereof.

Neither Houston nor his lawyer had any idea of the struggles that lay ahead.

* * *

Philip Newman called David Campbell as soon as he heard the news from Taylor Jones. Jones had set to work, first sending a request to Emory for Houston's records and then contacting Newman. Jones told Newman that Hunter Allen (Emory Clinic's attorney) had called him the same day Sargus Houston's request to release his records got to Emory. Hunter Allen had told Jones the staff caused the wrong eye to be operated on, but all had gone well. Dr. Newman told Campbell that there would definitely be a lawsuit.

The news shook Campbell through and through. Everyone in the department had known a lawsuit could happen; now it was real. He rocked back in his chair and reflected on the past few months. Not enough had happened—no follow-up to the Waring Committee report, no new investigation, nothing. The matter had been dropped.

Now there was a lawsuit, and David Campbell, despite his isolation, renewed his activities.

* * *

MARCH 1985

Taylor Jones had been working. He drafted a lawsuit after gathering records and interviewing as many people as he could. He wanted to surprise the Emory Clinic; he wanted to jar them, to shake things up. Since each partner could be held liable for the activities of the others, Jones wanted everyone to get a copy of the suit. He copied his lawsuit over a hundred times.

Late in this month the university business office called Dwight Cavanagh to say there was a deputy sheriff with lawsuits. Cavanagh scurried down to the ground level of the eye center and across to the main clinic building. There stood Deputy Sheriff Langley with a box stuffed with documents, and he planned to deliver a copy of the Houston suit to each and every clinic member. By this time Hunter Allen had arrived, and he conferred with Cavanagh, who worried that a lawsuit hand-delivered to every clinic doctor would ruin him. Allen needed to stop this now.

Hunter Allen was unruffled. A specialist in malpractice defense, he was well regarded in Atlanta and known for the aggressive defense of his clients. Allen, always dressed with coat and tie, had polite words for opponents and witnesses alike. Beneath the amiable exterior lay a bulldog, always guarding the welfare of his client. In short, Hunter Allen was an excellent and respected lawyer.

Hunter Allen recognized the combat tactics of a fellow litigator. Taylor Jones had thrown down the gauntlet. He was serving notice that Emory was in for a battle. The polite approach would have had Jones serving notice via a suit sent to Hunter Allen's office. Jones chose the opposite tack and almost succeeded in getting the lawsuits into each office. Hunter Allen calmed Dwight Cavanagh and sent him on his way. He took the suits from the deputy sheriff and dismissed him.

The suit named Cavanagh, Emory University Hospital, and the Emory Clinic as defendants. The charges included malpractice, negligence, battery, fraud, deception, and cover-up. Later amendments would add racketeering and other offenses. Taylor Jones never knew whether the individual doctors received their personal copies, but he made his point. He had declared war.

* * *

MARCH 5, 1985

Mattie Sue Brown introduced herself to Dr. Louis Wilson, her new ophthalmologist at Emory. Wilson spent a long time looking, re-looking, peering at the chart, and looking some more. He then told her that her left eye, the one that had not been operated upon, had a small cataract.

Brown wanted to know about the corneal problem also, and when would the transplant be done? Wilson told her that she did not need a transplant, that the eye had a normal cornea.

Mattie Brown protested that Cavanagh had told her she had a problem in both eyes, that both eyes would need a transplant. He had already transplanted that first cornea that he said was bad, and the eye still couldn't see and hurt her every day. Every day. What about that eye?

Wilson backed away from the slit lamp. He avoided Brown's question with a partial answer and a probing question of his own. That eye had a lot of astigmatism. It had an unusual shape, and the surface was rough. And why did she let him operate on that right eye?

Brown told Wilson that Cavanagh had talked like that eye would go blind without surgery.

Wilson pressed, "If I wanted to put you in a box and lock you up, would you let me?" Dr. Wilson's reply ended the discussion.

Brown's son Gerald had a private conversation with Wilson as his mother was checking out. Wilson would not comment on Mattie Sue's operated-upon eye, and he certainly did not tell Gerald that the pathology report on this eye showed no disease. But he did tell Gerald that Fuchs' dystrophy was a bilateral disease. If you had it in one eye, you would have it in the other. It didn't take Gerald Brown long to figure out the converse: if you didn't have it in one eye, you didn't have it in the other. Gerald Brown stalked out with a grim face.

* * *

March 8, 1985

Sargus Houston clutched his sister's arm as she maneuvered him into Dr. J.O. Martin's examining room. Houston hadn't seen Dr. Martin for two years, not since Martin had sent him to Cavanagh. When Taylor Jones met with Houston in late January, he had instructed Houston to cancel the February appointment with Dr. Cavanagh. When Jones later heard of Houston's poor vision, he recommended this March visit with Dr. Martin.

The technician instructed Houston to put his right hand on one arm of the exam chair and the left one on the other arm, then turn and sit down. He was then to cover the left eye and report the letters he saw.

Houston couldn't see any letters, not even the big ones. He could see three fingers with his right eye, he could just "zarn" (barely see) them.

Now he was to cover the right eye, and the left eye was tested. This eye, his former good eye, just barely saw a hand moving, no finger counting.

She recorded her findings as "count fingers right eye" and "hand motions left eye." Houston was blind.

Houston filled in Dr. Martin on the past two years.

He had been to Atlanta, where Martin had sent him. That doctor had done his good eye, and they told him the doctor decided to do it first. Then he had done his bad eye. He had been to Atlanta so many times he couldn't count. Last fall, Cavanagh had told him to come back in February, a couple of weeks ago. But then a man came to his niece's house and said that doctor made a mistake when he operated on his good eye. He meant to operate on his bad eye first, and they mixed it up and didn't tell him. He had hired a lawyer, attorney

Taylor Jones in Atlanta. As soon as he had told Jones he couldn't see, Jones told Houston to come see Dr. Martin.

Martin asked Houston about glaucoma, but Houston had never heard the word or been treated for it to his knowledge. Martin started Houston on treatment for glaucoma and told him to return in two weeks.

* * *

MARCH 8, 1985

Dr. Garland Perdue, now the CEO of the Emory Clinic, reviewed the notes in his file about Dwight Cavanagh. Perdue had met with Cavanagh and Hatcher in November, after receiving the Waring Committee's report. Perdue had felt that the corrective action of reducing and monitoring Dr. Cavanagh's practice had settled the matter. Yet he continued to hear of Campbell and Gammon's great unhappiness. Phrases like "cover-up," "lies," and "lack of character reform" came from numerous sources. This afternoon he was meeting with Campbell.

With the pleasantries over, it was time to get down to business. Campbell repeated all the issues to Perdue, especially the cover-up and the potential for a Medicare fraud investigation. Campbell felt that Perdue did not know all the problems, that new facts had come to light, that the administration hadn't acted on the Waring Committee report.

Perdue dictated the following as "Notes for the File":

I believed that corrective action rather than punitive action was desirable in the circumstances. Dr. Hatcher concurred. And it was our impression that the senior faculty of the department unanimously concurred. [Referring to the Waring Committee report].

In early March, 1985, it came to my attention that Drs. David Campbell and Allen Gammon were continuing to express dissatisfaction with the report.... I invited Dr. Campbell to my office for additional discussion. Dr. Campbell came to the office on Friday, March 8, and over a period of about two hours engaged in what, to me, was a rather nebulous expression of concern having to do with incomplete disclosure, uncertainty as to whether Dr. Cavanagh's character was any different, and whether we had met our ethical responsibility. At no time did Dr. Campbell furnish any new information, question the investigation of the previous allegation, define an appropriate reform in character, or indicate in any way where he thought ethics had been compromised. Dr. Campbell seemed to have the impression that I was unaware of the entire matter and frequently stated that he wanted to make sure that I knew everything. He did not propose any additional steps, indicating that he was satisfied with just making sure it was all known. In response to my questioning, however, he did indicate that there was a range of support of Dr. Cavanagh within the department, indicating that there was some strong support, but others very negative, and leaving the impression that he felt the majority did not offer support. I inquired whether "this represented a crisis in confidence in leadership," and he replied in the affirmative. I then suggested a meeting with the department to address this issue and any others that might be related, and Dr. Campbell enthusiastically agreed. I informed Dr. Hatcher and Dr. Cavanagh and called a meeting of the department for the evening of Monday, March 18. With the consent of the members present, I did ask Mr. Hunter Allen to be present, since I had been led to believe by Dr. Campbell that the specific incident should be discussed further as well.

It is necessary here to detail certain impressions. Throughout his original conversation with me, Dr. Campbell gave credence to the already existent rumor that one or more individuals within the department would encourage and collaborate with litigation initiated on behalf of the patient; that information would be made known to other ophthalmologists, organizations of ophthalmologists, the press and the public. Dr. Campbell frequently indicated that he would not be the one to do this; that he didn't know who would do it, but that he was confident that it would occur. In many instances, the conversation took the tone of what I had to interpret as veiled threats, only to be subsequently contradicted by statements that he wouldn't do it. Dr. Campbell would make such comments as "when this is known..., when the lawyers find out..., when this gets out in the community..., etc., etc. ".

David Campbell knew the faculty meeting with Perdue would be crucial. Here are his thoughts as he prepared himself on Sunday, March 17:

Sunday morning.... Beware the Ides of March. I now feel as this spring comes that the issue is over, that I am over with it, that my emotional, terrible turmoil has come to an end, that my resolution that I would act to put a stop to the harmful care to patients and that I would act appropriately in regard to notification of the medical school has come to pass, and that I can now, having talked with Garland Perdue, be at peace with myself, feeling that I have done all I could do to put a stop to this horrible business.

So David Campbell, hopeful of support from more in the department than Allen Gammon, relieved that the affair would be over but somewhat nervous about Monday's meeting, waited for the appointed hour.

MARCH 18, 1985

Garland Perdue's notes provide his version of the eye department's meeting:

At the outset of the meeting I explained the reason for Mr. [Hunter] Allen's presence, and the ophthalmologists present unanimously agreed that he should be. I also indicated that Dr. Cavanagh was willing to sit in on the meeting or be excused from the entire meeting. All present invited him to stay. I then reminded them that he could be excused at any time, for any reason, but at no time during the meeting was such a request made by any individual. The entire senior faculty attended, with the exception of Dr. Gammon, who had indicated that he accorded a higher priority to a meeting of the Quality Assurance Committee of Egleston Hospital [Emory's children's hospital].

There was frank and open discussion, which I directed toward the questions of whether the previous inquiry had been adequate, whether there was support for the findings and conclusions, and whether there was continued confidence in the effectiveness of leadership. All present spoke in varying lengths, including Dr. Campbell, who repeated most of his previous assertions. All those present were unanimous in affirming strong support for the adequacy of the inquiry, the appropriateness of the conclusions and recommendations, the appropriateness of the actions taken, and strong confidence in the quality of leadership. They further expressed strong confidence in the composition and quality of the members of the section, and their strong belief that no further action was indicated, provided the oversight report was furnished as requested. After some hours, the review of the state of the section seemed incomplete, and I volunteered to reconvene the meeting the following evening for a continued discussion.

At this meeting [the following evening, March 19] *Dr. Gammon did attend and was invited to speak along with the others. Most of Dr. Gammon's statements seemed to revolve around his personal concern as to whether he could achieve tenure and carry on with his self-perceived outstanding work. Comments directed to Dr. Gammon and Dr. Campbell from other members of the faculty could be perceived as excoriating. Both were asked if they were the sources of outside communication rumored to have occurred.... Each denied he was the source. Ultimately, others in the meeting raised the question as to whether they were not themselves showing a lack of ethics, demonstrating disruptive behavior, and failing to carry out their own academic and clinical responsibilities to the maximum degree. Well into the meeting, it appeared that all the questions had been resolved. Dr. Campbell and Dr. Gammon indicated their acceptance of the outcome and their continued support for the department's leadership and their belief that all issues had been resolved. At that point I was informed that the department members would wish to continue their discussion about internal matters relating to future developments in the department, and the meeting related to the inquiry and the confidence in leadership was completed. I accepted the assurances from Drs. Campbell and Gammon that all matters had been resolved to their satisfaction, and that no further action need be undertaken.*

Again, it is necessary to record personal impressions: Dr. Cavanagh was largely silent and in no way attempted to influence the course of the discussion. He was not asked to leave at any time; he therefore heard all of the positive and negative statements made by all parties and made no rejoinder. I had the further impression that the rest of the department considered Dr. Campbell and Dr. Gammon to be completely out of line in continuing to raise the issue. The other members present expressed complete confidence in Dr. Cavanagh, and allowed the inference, if not actually stated, of lack of confidence in Dr. Campbell and Dr. Gammon. Since everyone present chose to speak at length and without any apparent inhibitions, this certainly gave the impression of participatory democracy. Near the end, it also gave the impression of group therapy.

The salient features of the meeting were discussed with Dr. Hatcher.

So much for David Campbell's hope for support. But Campbell's conscience was clear after speaking up. He thought he was through with this mess. Allen Gammon, not intimidated, knew more battles lay ahead.

MARCH 21, 1985

Dignitaries and donors gathered under a spring sun to dedicate the new Emory Eye Center. I was part of the audience that sat on small metal chairs under an intense blue sky, looking up at the stage where Cavanagh, Laney, and others had gathered. But it was the new eye center that commanded the eye. The handsome building impressed us all with an inner atrium that spanned all five floors. It had its own outpatient operating suite on the lowest floor. The architecture, design, and décor were sleek and modern.

Cavanagh spoke of life being a journey as he had in his memo of the previous summer. He referred to the new center as a way station along a continuous journey. University president James Laney drew laughter when he responded that he hoped the eye center represented more than just a way station, and there wouldn't be another trip like the one in getting the center built. Department chairmen from across the country spoke, praising Emory and Cavanagh. The faculty was front and center, a happy family as far as guests knew. No one could tell that a lawsuit had been served a few weeks earlier and a bitter two nights had divided them just days before. Garland Perdue's thought that the faculty was in agreement proved to be dead wrong.

* * *

MARCH 31, 1985

John Wright, the pathologist, left Emory on this day, exhausted by the lack of support from Cavanagh and disputes within the faculty. He joined a private group in Atlanta. The tissue committee had never reviewed the Code 3 reports sent to them by Wright. He later would testify that he heard that they were "too busy" to review his concerns.

APRIL 1985

The letter from John O. Martin, Sargus Houston's doctor in Macon, arrived late in the month as Cavanagh prepared for the annual Georgia Society of Ophthalmology's meeting.

April 23, 1985

Dear Dwight,

We saw Mr. Houston on 3/8/85, at which time he said his left eye was about gone.... Best corrected vision at this time was finger count in the right eye and hand motion in the left eye.

The patient has marked optic nerve atrophy. At his last visit, on 3/22/85, the findings were the same, but his pressure had decreased to 22 in the right eye and 20 in the left eye.

I am sorry to give you such a dismal report, but I am afraid this is what he has gotten himself into.

If I can help in any way please call.

Cordially,
John O. Martin, M.D.

This letter was the first indication that Sargus Houston was blind. Dr. Cavanagh and Hunter Allen conferred about a plan to obtain an independent evaluation.

* * *

MAY 1985

Georgia's ophthalmologists loved springtime. The best, the most luxurious, and the most leisurely meeting of the year brought them to the Georgia coast in early May. The Georgia Society of Ophthalmology, the GSO, met on Sea Island at the exclusive old Cloister Hotel, Georgia's only five-star resort. Sea Island, on the Atlantic Ocean with vast marshes on its west side, was covered with huge live oak trees draped with Spanish moss. Tradition ruled here—coat and tie at night, no name tags in the lobby, peace and discretion at all times.

Here the state's ophthalmologists gathered to hear famous speakers bring everyone up-to-date on the latest techniques and procedures. The leadership met to plot political strategy against its perennial enemies, the optometrists. For years, the less-well-trained, non–M.D. rivals had levered their political connections so that the state legislatures granted optometry increasing medical privileges, placing not only patients at risk, but to some degree physicians' incomes as well.

Other games played out beneath the surface. The untrained eye could look at the serene marsh waters and totally miss the life-and-death struggles beneath, which only occasionally rippled the surface. In a similar way, a naïve eye, looking at the intent audience, the scurrying and visiting of vendors' booths during the breaks and the pleasantries at the cocktail parties, would miss the struggles amongst the doctors. Only these struggles didn't involve life and death as in the marsh. The doctors battled over money and power.

The educated eye could see it all. Subspecialists from Georgia's two academic centers worked the general ophthalmologists, shoring up relations, hoping to keep the flow of referrals pouring into their offices. Young subspecialists in private practice would do the same, hoping to steal referring sources and wean them away from the academic centers. The politically active doctors hustled for recognition and votes, planning their moves up the ladder of organized medicine. The vendors and drug reps gave out as many trinkets as they could, desperate to keep doctors using their drugs, lens implants, and other devices. The current leaders, accountable for legislative victories and losses, would parade around the visiting legislative dignitary, exhorting against the apathy of the typical doc, who did nothing to assure victory in the statehouse but was quick to criticize the lack of results when the inevitable losses came in.

Against this backdrop of the usual battles, the Emory doctors waged their own war. Dwight Cavanagh, charming as always, worked his way through the crowd, aware that many of the attendees knew of his wrong-eye surgery. He could watch and count up his support by noting who spent time with Campbell or Gammon in intense head-bowed, private conferences. Campbell had been nominated for president of the GSO, and the confirmatory vote would take place at the meeting of the Council, the board of the GSO.

Meanwhile, those talking to Campbell had different messages. There was a huge mess at Emory. Why hasn't something been done? How can Emory keep him on when his own faculty has cut back his practice and has to monitor his charts? How can that be? Campbell kept his head bowed for reasons other than the desire for privacy. He bowed his head in shame, shame and frustration at the inaction on his campus.

One of Campbell's allies had more status than the others. He invited Campbell to walk along the marsh for a private conversation. Dr. Irving Staley had practiced in Marietta, a suburb of Atlanta, for years. He was one of ten physicians on the Composite State Board of Medical Examiners. He let Campbell know he was inquiring on behalf of the state board, not as a curious private ophthalmologist.

Staley grilled Campbell on the disturbing rumors about Cavanagh, and Campbell related the events of the past two years, including the recent faculty meeting with Garland Perdue. Campbell concluded with his own observations that it seemed Emory's administration had done all it planned to do. Perdue and Hatcher had met with Dwight; they knew his practice had been cut back; they knew Lou Wilson was monitoring his charts. Dr. Perdue had said that corrective, not punitive, action was warranted. Dwight Cavanagh was being sued. Dr. Campbell hadn't seen any change in behavior. Cavanagh was still operating, with Wilson looking at charts not patients.

Dr. Staley told Campbell that the board would conduct its own investigation unless Emory did more. He wanted Campbell to send this message to the administration.

That afternoon Campbell attended the Council meeting where he anticipated a vote confirming his nomination as the president-elect of the society. Instead, another doctor's name was nominated and confirmed. Campbell, deeply embarrassed, quietly left the room. All eyes gazed elsewhere, no one willing to acknowledge his presence or his leaving.

The presidency of the GSO was an honor—not a lot of work, and an honor accorded to good doctors who had worked hard for the society. He assumed that Dwight Cavanagh had sabotaged his candidacy, given Cavanagh's capacity for retribution and infighting. He also had no doubt about his own stance on the issue. He knew he was correct and that he would keep fighting, even if it meant his career at Emory.

At the evening cocktail party, held on the lawn beneath the huge live oaks draped with Spanish moss, Campbell ran into Emory's head orthoptist, Frankie Stegall. She evaluated patients for many of Atlanta's private ophthalmologists and was a pipeline into the community. She had already heard about Campbell's lost presidency. If Campbell was looking for sympathy, he had come to the wrong person.

She told him the reason he lost out was not Dwight Cavanagh, but himself, that he'd been pushing criticism of Cavanagh so hard that the sympathy had shifted to Dwight. She said that people felt Campbell was forcing them to make a choice, and that they were mad at him, not Cavanagh. She warned Campbell that he and Allen Gammon needed to watch out. They needed to back off.

* * *

MAY 1985

Genevieve Switz, no longer working in the eye department, tried three times to put the key in the ignition. Her hands trembled and her eyes blurred. She drove home on automatic pilot, not noticing red lights or traffic. She sped straight to her husband, and her fears tumbled out. Still trembling, unable to sit, she unloaded the evening's events and later testified to these in her deposition. She told how she had met with Hunter Allen and an insurance man at the clinic's cafeteria. They did everything but tell her they would sue her. They knew she had copies of patient charts, and they said it was illegal for her to have them.

They also knew about the African-American patients being operated on at the end of the day and questioned her about that. They thought she was the one who tipped off Sargus Houston's lawyer. Mr. Allen was sure there was a mole and was intent on finding out who it might be. They suspected both Switz and Newman.

And then, at the end, Hunter Allen said that he would represent Switz if anything came up, and that she'd better not meet with Houston's lawyer unless Allen or the insurance man was with her. Hunter Allen also told her that he had talked with Dr. Cavanagh right after the wrong-eye case, and Allen told her, "I told him what to do, but I didn't think he would do such a bungling job of it." Switz realized the threat implicit in the meeting, and she didn't know how to protect herself.

After further consultation, Switz wrote Hunter Allen a letter telling him that if he requested the chart copies she had, she would most likely comply with his request.

* * *

After hearing of Sargus Houston's blindness, Hunter Allen had called Houston's attorney, Taylor Jones, and offered to pay for an independent examination and treatment for Houston anywhere in the country or in Atlanta. Jones chose to send Houston to me, and Sargus Houston came to my office on May 13, now a year and eight months after the wrong-eye surgery.

I, like most ophthalmologists in Atlanta, had heard of the wrong-eye surgery, but I didn't know the particulars. Sargus Houston related to me that he had gone to Emory for poor vision in his right eye, but that the left eye was the one that had been operated on. He offered no details on why the left eye was operated on, but he did note that this eye had never seen well after the surgery, and as of a few months ago, both eyes were quite impaired. He was taking a drop to treat glaucoma and a steroid drop to fight inflammation, both given by his Macon doctor.

Sitting in front of me was a simple man, obviously of limited means, whose daily activities did not require clear vision from both eyes.

What does it mean to be blind? First, most "blind" patients are not totally blind, and the term "visually impaired" is more accurate. The spectrum of visual impairment ranges from the frustrating inability to read, drive, and function to total lack of light perception in both eyes. The public fears blindness second only to cancer, and rightly so. You are removed from the ability to live life as you want, especially if you enjoy reading or other activities that require keen sight. You become dependent on others and on cumbersome visual aids. Your life slows down, and you do less. Yet over time people adjust to this impairment as they do to many others, and their lives become tolerable.

Sargus Houston was at the far end of the spectrum of blindness, where dependence on others is maximal and independence is minimal. He could see a hand move with his right eye and no light with his left. The surgery performed by Cavanagh looked reasonably good, in that the corneas were clear; the angle, the area of fluid drainage, free of scarring; the pressure was normal and the lens implants were clear. He was not blind because of a transplant gone bad or a slipped or defective implant; he was blind because he had optic-nerve changes classic for glaucoma, deep and extensive "cupping." Once a nerve has reached this stage, the changes are permanent. If he had not developed glaucoma, or if he had been diagnosed and treated, he would have been able to function normally.

How had he developed glaucoma, and how long had it been going on? In Houston's specific case, as in many others', Cavanagh's chart provides no clue. Glaucoma is a slow disease and almost never blinds an eye in a matter of weeks unless the pressure is markedly elevated. Houston's niece had noted his decreasing vision in the fall of 1984, but he had insisted that he could see well and told me that he could read as late as Christmas, a year and three months after his surgery.

In the eventual legal wrangling, Hunter Allen would repeatedly blame Taylor Jones for Houston's blindness, stating that Jones had instructed Houston to leave Cavanagh's care. Hunter Allen asserted that if the scheduled appointment had been kept, Sargus Houston would not have gone blind. But Houston had not been scheduled to see Cavanagh until February 1985, five months after his last appointment. Houston saw J.O. Martin in March, only one month after the cancelled appointment with Cavanagh. Glaucoma is a slow and insidious disease, and glaucoma, not Taylor Jones, blinded Sargus Houston.

Unfortunately I could not help this man, except to maintain treatment to keep the small amount of peripheral vision in his right eye. My other duty was for the attorney. Officially, I had performed an "IME," an Independent Medical Evaluation, and I owed a report to Taylor Jones so he could prepare his case. I sent the report and continued Houston's treatment.

* * *

David Campbell returned to his tape recorder in June:

June 22, 1985—Saturday

I had a talk with Philip Newman this week and a talk with Tom Harbin this week and have learned some remarkable new facts. Phil was rather frank with me about the details surrounding the event of the wrong eye and the attempt by Dwight to blame it on Phil...Phil also said there were multiple copies of the record [Sargus Houston's chart, which he and Switz were convinced had been altered by someone else].

Phil then told me an astounding fact that he had not told me before, and that was that he and Genevieve overheard Dwight lie to the patient on the first postoperative day when they all walked into the room together, and the patient said, "Hey, Doc, I thought you were going to operate on the other eye," and Dwight said to the patient, "No, we changed our minds and decided to operate on this eye first."

My position once was to put a stop to the harmful behavior to patients, notify the university, and demand a complete change in Dwight. But the two things [that Cavanagh had lied to Houston and that Houston was blind] *that I have learned this spring that now make me feel that Dwight should not remain as chairman, and this is the first time I have felt this, are that first, he was* [lying], *that the monumentality of the lying in regard to the cover-up in this case is such that I feel a man who was willing to lie and cover-up in the postoperative period is not the kind of man who should be a departmental chairman.... It is very clear to me now that Dwight is going to fall and that I now feel that he should, and that I am going to take every step that I can to try and put the university into the appropriate posture. I'm also going to make the prediction that this will all become public, that the headlines will be unbearable, and that if the university does not act before this becomes public, they are going to be badly smeared. And, this is what I'm going to tell the president. I will tell the president that Dwight has many enemies, and that I have been told that this is all going to get into the newspapers, that there is activity at the level of the State Board of Medical Examiners, that there is activity at the level of the Georgia Society of Ophthalmology, and there is activity and a general distrust in the community of Dr. Cavanagh.*

And, having told everyone this and made these predictions, if I'm wrong, I leave, but I'm in a situation now where I have to leave anyway, so I have absolutely nothing to lose and, perhaps, something to gain, and I do the right thing, morally and ethically.... And I have given strong thoughts to elsewhere and strong thoughts to returning to New England....

* * *

JULY 1985

So, once again, David Campbell began making the rounds of Emory's administrative hierarchy. First was the chairman of the Department of Surgery, Dr. Dean Warren, and Campbell dictated the following:

July 1, 1985. I just went over and had a talk with Dean Warren, the head of surgery, whose office is in the hospital, so I guess he is the head of surgery at Emory.... When I went in, he had me sit next to him at his desk, not across the desk, and I think that's an important thing to do for people.... And I told him about the wrong-eye case. He said no one had informed him from our department about it, that he had heard about it from Garland Perdue, and that the general story was that, yes, the wrong eye had been done, but that both eyes were about the same, and it didn't make much difference which eye had been done.

He knew nothing else about the problems that Dwight had except that he'd heard some vague rumors.... I talked about the wrong-eye case, told him the real story, that one eye was a 20/25 eye, the other eye was a 20/200 eye, that the eye that was 20/25 was now blind, in fact the patient was blind... that the family had been lied to, and that Dwight had been overheard in that lie....

And I told him that I was thinking of leaving, that there had been a lot of strain put on me over the past couple of years....

The next stop for Dr. Campbell was Charles Hatcher, who received him none too pleasantly. He told Campbell that Dr. Garland Perdue kept him informed, that he knew about the March faculty meeting and the huge discussion. He had heard that only Allen Gammon agreed with Campbell. Everybody else supported Dwight. Campbell agreed that everyone else had supported Cavanagh, but only because Cavanagh was right there listening.

Dr. Hatcher asked Campbell if he had anything new. New facts, new problems?

Campbell's dictated notes summarize the time spent with Charlie Hatcher: *So I walked out of there in conclusion feeling that no moral or ethical issue is going to touch the man, that only financial issues talk, and that the only impression I made was in getting him to realize the seriousness of the financial situation [lawsuit].... As I walked out the door, there was no comment, no statement he would take care of things or that I would hear from him.*

* * *

July 16, 1985

Dr. Charles Hatcher
The Emory Clinic

Dear Dr. Hatcher:

The purpose of this letter is to avoid misunderstanding and to state my position in regard to the current matters of concern in the Department of Ophthalmology. I feel that an inquiry should determine the truth and seriousness of the matter. Following this, decisions should be made by senior officials in regard to future course. Until the truth and seriousness of these matters have been fully established, I advocate no one solution to this problem. My hope is that a solution can be found that will uphold the integrity of the department and the university. Further, I hope that the solution will provide justice to those involved as well as limitation of possible harm to both the department, the university, and to all individuals involved.

Sincerely,
David G. Campbell, M.D.

A copy of this letter went to Perdue, Dean Warren, and the eye faculty.

David Campbell's letter to Charles Hatcher infuriated his fellow eye faculty. Travis Meredith barged in soon after reading the letter and warned Campbell to read his Machiavelli, especially the part about killing the king, or trying to. If you are after the king, you'd better kill him, or you get killed yourself. Louis Wilson was even less subtle. He had a small piece of cord in his hands, looped into a noose. As he and Campbell talked, Wilson kept tightening the noose around his index finger. Tightening and loosing, tightening and loosing. David Campbell got the picture.

* * *

JULY 17, 1985

When doctors fight, lawyers feast. The delivery of Sargus Houston's lawsuit set a table that fattened many Atlanta attorneys for years. The appetizer course, the first deposition, was served in downtown Atlanta on this hot, humid July day at 2:00 PM. Peachtree Center's twin towers soared above a subway station and food court in the northernmost part of Atlanta's downtown congregation of large buildings. The office of Hunter S. Allen Jr., Esq. was located at 2222 Peachtree Center Tower.

Gathering this afternoon were Michael Bennett, Esq., representing the defendant, Emory University Hospital; Taylor Jones, Esq., representing the plaintiff, Sargus Houston; and Hunter Allen, who represented both the Emory Clinic and Dwight Cavanagh. The attorneys, all of whom had offices near Allen's, walked over. Dwight Cavanagh, the first person to undergo a deposition, drove in from nearby Decatur.

Civil litigation is highly ritualized warfare fought with rigid rules defined by numerous court cases. One of the rules concerns "discovery," a process in which each side asks the other for all documents related to a lawsuit. An element of discovery is the deposition, the opportunity to grill each potential witness, as well as each defendant and plaintiff, under oath before a trial. A court reporter transcribes everything asked and answered, or not answered, according to the dictate of the attorneys. When all depositions are completed and documents produced, the attorneys can judge the strength of both sides of the case, assess the impact on a jury, and either go ahead with a trial or settle without a trial.

Lawyers also get the chance to assess the credibility and impact of the witnesses. Even when a witness is experienced in depositions, immediately before a new one, the attorney will sit him down and remind him of the rules. On this day, Hunter Allen's instructions would have gone like this: "Now Dwight, listen to the question. Let him finish asking the question and then answer just what he asked, and only if I don't object. He may ask you questions that I don't want answered. If he does, I will tell you not to answer. When you're answering, don't volunteer anything, nothing. Only answer what he asks and no more. If you don't know, say so. Stick to the subject; don't give him any ammunition. Remember, you're under oath. I know you would only tell the truth, but remember, if you say something that isn't true, that's perjury. Everything you say can be brought up during the trial."

For five hours Taylor Jones and Dwight Cavanagh went back and forth, painfully going over all the details of Houston's chart, his first visit, and the surgery. Cavanagh testified that he told both the patient and his sister that he did not operate on the eye he "intended" to operate on. In regard to Cavanagh's opinion of Philip Newman, he said, "At that point in time, an error, having been committed, it didn't do any good to start blaming people. That's not my style."

Jones asked Cavanagh if he knew whether or not David Campbell had prepared a narrative of the Houston episode and the committee investigation, and further, if Cavanagh was aware of whether or not Dr. Campbell had recently gone to one or more members of the board of trustees. Cavanagh knew nothing of either question.

Allen instructed Cavanagh not to answer the numerous questions about the committee investigation, and the deposition finally ended at 7:00.

Hunter Allen must have paid as close attention to the questions not asked as the ones asked. He had attended the previous department meetings and had reviewed the Waring Committee report. While Allen was not about to let any witness answer questions about material covered in peer-protected proceedings, he must have wondered how much Jones knew, how much the campus moles had told him. In this opening round, Jones had stuck to questions about Houston and his care. If he knew about other issues, he didn't ask. Allen and Cavanagh had to wonder about Campbell's activities and involvement with Jones, given the questions at the end. But there must have been relief at the absence of questions about unnecessary surgery, fraudulent billing, and neglected blind eyes of the undiscovered glaucoma patients. A host of depositions lay ahead.

* * *

July 22, 1985

Dr. David Campbell
Department of Ophthalmology

Dear David:
Following our conversation last week, I met with Drs. Louis Wilson, Henry Kaplan, Robert Spector, and talked at

length by telephone with Dr. Travis Meredith. None of these individuals support your allegations against Dr. Cavanagh and they all feel that the professional audit performed last year was definitive and that the issue need not be reopened. I might add that they are somewhat distressed about your continued activity against Dr. Cavanagh and feel that it is taking on all the tones of a personal vendetta.

I have written Dr. Garland Perdue...and asked that he refer the audit for review by the Professional Standards and Ethics Committee....

In the meantime, I feel that it is appropriate to confine your (charges) to facts which you can subsequently support without question, otherwise rumors and distortions will cause unnecessary harm to you, Dr. Cavanagh, and the Department of Ophthalmology.

Sincerely,
Charles R. Hatcher, Jr., M.D.

* * *

David Campbell met with president James Laney on July 23. In a later deposition, Laney would describe Campbell as agitated and depressed, dour in appearance. While acknowledging that Campbell brought up all the issues relating to Dwight Cavanagh, Laney testified that his previous knowledge of Cavanagh was "most laudatory. He was lionized and worshipped by people." Campbell remembered Laney's promise to convene a select "blue-ribbon" committee of outside experts; Laney could remember no such promise.

At any rate, Laney referred the matter back to Hatcher and took no independent action.

* * *

JULY 29, 1985

Dr. Louis Wilson operated on Mattie Sue Brown, an uneventful cataract extraction and lens implantation on her left eye. This eye did well, but she remained miserable from the pain and blurred vision in her right eye. She and her family realized that this left eye did not have Fuchs' disease and did not need a corneal transplant. They were also fairly sure the first eye had no corneal disease. Wilson hadn't come out and said it, but he might as well have. Unsophisticated as they may have been in eye disease, they both knew the source of her misery was the corneal transplant, not the cataract surgery. She and her son brooded on the misdiagnosis.

* * *

AUGUST 1985

"Seabrook, it's Johnny Anonymous for you."

Charles Seabrook, science and medicine writer for the *Atlanta Journal-Constitution*, Atlanta's morning newspaper, picked up the phone.

Did Mr. Seabrook know that there was a lawsuit against the chairman of ophthalmology at Emory?

Well, no, Seabrook didn't know that. But he did know who the chairman was. Four years earlier, Seabrook had written an article about a local ophthalmologist who had been among the first to perform a new type of eye surgery, radial keratotomy (RK). At that time, RK was relatively crude and unproven. Private ophthalmologists had taken the lead, advertising the new RK surgery before academic ophthalmologists had researched and approved it. George Waring, other academic corneal specialists, the Georgia Society of Ophthalmology, and the American Academy of Ophthalmology had all pushed for a moratorium on the procedure until a multicenter study, funded by the National Eye Institute, could prove

RK's effectiveness and safety. The private ophthalmologists had responded with a class-action lawsuit against Waring, Emory, and many other defendants. Seabrook's article appeared three years ago as these events were transpiring.

The day after the 1982 article was published, Waring and Cavanagh had called Seabrook. They "raked me over the coals," recalled Seabrook. Seabrook had previously written on the legislative battles between ophthalmology and optometry and had kept the public aware as the RK study and lawsuit progressed. So he was familiar not only with the battles of ophthalmology, but with some of the players as well. He had heard rumors of Dr. Cavanagh's troubles at Emory but none of the facts.

After Johnny Anonymous had finished telling about the current problems, Seabrook got to work. He obtained a copy of the lawsuit and began making phone calls.

* * *

As promised by Dr. Hatcher, another Emory committee was to investigate the Cavanagh affair. It would be a standing committee, the Professional Standards and Ethics Committee of the Emory Clinic, headed by Dr. George Tindall, chairman of the Neurosurgery Department. The letter from Garland Perdue gave the charge to the committee:

August 2, 1985

George Tindall, M.D.
Chairman
Professional Standards and Ethics Committee
Neurosurgery
The Emory Clinic

Dear George,

This letter is to verify the charge given to your committee at the meeting on August 1st.

Your committee was requested to evaluate the circumstances leading to the current controversy regarding the section of ophthalmology. I provided certain background information to the effect that an incident in which the incorrect eye of a patient was operated upon led to the formation of a select committee of professors in the Department of Ophthalmology to conduct an investigation of this matter, as well as related allegations of other improper practices. The investigation was completed, and conclusions and recommendations were concurred by the seven senior faculty members in the department [section]. The report was furnished to Dr. Hatcher, who forwarded the report to me to take further action.

I confirmed the findings and recommendations by individual interviews with Drs. Wilson, Kaplan, Meredith, and Stulting. While the report indicated that medical care by Dr. H. Dwight Cavanagh exhibited a "standard of care on occasion inappropriate for this department," it was their belief that none of the inappropriate activities were the result of misconduct, incompetence, or fraudulent activities.

I discussed this with you and others and with your concurrence, the following actions were taken:

1. *Dr. Cavanagh was to reduce his operative case load and his outpatient case load.*

2. *He was to intensify efforts to see patients in a timely manner and take the appropriate administrative steps to ensure appropriate patient flow and timely appointments.*

3. *He was to pay appropriate increased attention to accuracy in documentation, clear statements of indications for surgery, and documentation of the steps of management of his patients.*

4. *He was to submit his practice to oversight and monitoring by Dr. Louis Wilson, the senior ophthalmic surgeon in the Emory Clinic.*

It has been reported to me that the oversight has been completely satisfactory. In spite of the investigation and the report of this oversight, Drs. Allen Gammon and David Campbell continue to raise questions that the allegations of inappropriate activities were not satisfactorily resolved. Additionally, confidence in leadership within the Section was questioned. As a further effort to resolve these questions, I met with Dr. Campbell to hear his statement and then met with members of the section on two successive evenings to hear statements from all members of the section of ophthalmology. All other members of the section of ophthalmology refuted Campbell and Gammon, and indicated their strong support for the investigation, its conclusions and recommendations, and for the actions which had been taken. Additionally, they expressed strong support for continued leadership by Dr. Cavanagh. Drs. Campbell and Gammon indicated their acceptance, but in recent weeks have recanted their acceptance.

I therefore asked you to rehear the matter and arrive at answers to the following questions:

1. *Was the original investigation adequate and correct?*
2. *Should the investigation be reopened?*
3. *Were the actions taken by the clinic director responsible and correct?*
4. *Is there evidence of* **current** [emphasis added] *impropriety in the section of ophthalmology?*
5. *Is Dr. Cavanagh, the section head, fit to continue in office?*
6. *Has Dr. Campbell acted responsibly and correctly?*
7. *Has Dr. Gammon acted responsibly and correctly?*

8. *Do you recommend further action, including disciplinary action, to resolve this matter?*

I am conscious and appreciative.... I reiterate that it is our joint concern to ascertain that the professional standards, ethical standards, and integrity of the Emory Clinic are preserved.

Sincerely,
Garland D. Perdue, M.D.
Clinic Director

Most ethics committee meetings are small, private affairs, with only the physician members and those being investigated attending. This investigation was different. Also attending would be Hunter Allen, the Emory Clinic attorney; Roy Townsend, the executive administrator of the clinic; and a court reporter who would transcribe all testimony. Instead of an intimate, truth-gathering investigation, the Tindall Committee would resemble a formal court hearing. For the first time, David Campbell and Allen Gammon were the subjects of inquiry, not just Dwight Cavanagh. The first meeting was set for August 5.

* * *

SUNDAY, AUGUST 4, 1985

The Atlanta Journal-Constitution surprised the Emory campus on this weekend morning:

"BRILLIANT" EMORY EYE SURGEON UNDER INVESTIGATION
By Charles Seabrook, Science/Medicine Writer

Allegations of unnecessary surgery, altered patient records and overcharging for medical care at Emory University's Eye Clinic are being investigated by the institution's standards and ethics committee, Emory officials revealed Friday.

The investigation centers around Dr. H. Dwight Cavanagh, chairman of Emory's Ophthalmology Department, who has been described as one of the nation's most brilliant eye surgeons.

Cavanagh has also been named in a medical malpractice suit, accusing him of operating on the wrong eye of a patient and then trying to cover it up by altering the patient's medical records. In court records, Cavanagh acknowledges operating on the wrong eye but denies that he changed any medical files.

The Emory investigation was prompted by the complaints of at least two eye doctors within the Ophthalmology Department. The doctors went to medical school officials and said they suspected Cavanagh had performed unnecessary surgery, altered patient records and overcharged patients for certain types of procedures.

Cavanagh denies any wrongdoing and said that he is the victim of professional jealousy.

"I have been through a lot," Cavanagh said. "I have lost many nights' sleep to figure out why they're making these unsubstantiated charges against me."

Two previous investigations by other Emory committees found no evidence of intentional wrongdoing at the clinic, although several other problems, including sloppy record-keeping and delays in treating patients were found....

* * *

Gerald Brown, Mattie Sue's son, jumped into action after reading Seabrook's article. He called his sister in Columbus, who was keeping Mattie Sue as she recovered from Dr. Louis Wilson's cataract surgery. Mattie Sue was not to see that article. In her shape, there was no telling what she would do. The sister was to hide that newspaper. Gerald would handle things from here.

Later he called Seabrook. He wanted the name of that lawyer, the one who sued Cavanagh. He related that, after her 1982 operation, he had seen her go from an active person to one that "set" in a rocking chair, cried, and had no desire to get involved in any activities. He saw her go from being an active person and a healthy person to someone who was totally concerned with only one thing: her eye. It was her total conversation with everybody she spoke to. Now, exactly who was that lawyer?

* * *

AUGUST 5, 1985

George Tindall waved a copy of the *AJC* article as he passed out copies to his ethics committee. The article added a layer of anger to a room already simmering; most of the seven committee members had cancelled summer vacations to go into this emergency session. Tindall realized full well their feelings, but he had his orders.

The transcript shows that after Tindall called the meeting to order, he pointed out that the article added urgency and importance to their deliberations. There was no coincidence between the timing of the article and their meeting. The mole was at work.

Tindall introduced the guests—Hunter Allen, Roy Townsend, and the court reporter. The first testimony came from Garland Perdue, Emory Clinic's director. Perdue read his charge to the committee and added his own comments. He expressed his frustration that Campbell and Gammon had recanted their acceptance of Cavanagh's leadership soon after the March faculty meetings. Perdue made it clear that residents from other departments were well aware of the situation in the eye department and had heard of cover-up, fraud, and altered records. He noted that the integrity of the entire campus leadership had come into question.

Next came Cavanagh's inner circle—Drs. Louis Wilson, Travis Meredith, and Hank Kaplan—the executive committee of the eye department. Meredith began by detailing the outside responsibilities taken on by Cavanagh as he built the busiest corneal practice in the world and raised $10 million dollars ($22 million in 2008 dollars) for the eye center. These included serving as secretary-treasurer of the Association for Research in Vision and Ophthalmology, Chairman of the National Institutes of Health study section, Secretary of the American Academy's Governmental Regulatory Affairs subcommittee, member of the Board of Councilors of the Contact Lens Association of America, and Council of the Georgia Society of Ophthalmology.

Meredith continued as he summarized the Houston case: *The very regrettable incident that happened in the operating room in 1983 was that a patient with bilateral disease, bilateral progressive corneal dystrophy, was scheduled for surgery in one eye and inadvertently had surgery in another eye. Interestingly, the patient retained sufficient confidence...to return and allow Dr. Cavanagh to operate on the other eye some months later.*

Of the chart alterations, Meredith noted: *There were problems in the charts with some changes in the chart that were write-overs of material gained by the technicians.... These were questions of changes in vision and changes of pressure. This is certainly a legitimate thing to do, to change material that's obtained by a technician; but we urged him...that if he were to make a change in the chart to strike over that and initial the change himself.*

Tindall interrupted: *Was there a perception that the values were changed to make the person a more suitable candidate for surgery?*

To which Meredith replied: *It was my impression and opinion that these changes, while they were not desirable and could be interpreted in that light, did not constitute anything that was clearly, clearly unethical and did not constitute any clear evidence of wrongdoing.*

The meeting dragged on for hours as the Waring Committee report was dissected and discussed and opinions were given in defense of Cavanagh. In the case of the misdiagnosed Fuchs' cases, in which no pathology had been found, including Mattie Sue Brown, now Wilson's patient, Wilson commented, *So it would be very difficult to say in these cases where there wasn't clear histopathology whether the surgery was inappropriate.*

Later Wilson would remind the committee, *Let me remind you that the patient* [Sargus Houston] *had bilateral disease. It was a matter of degree as to which eye would be done first.*

After defending Cavanagh, attention turned to Campbell and Gammon. Kaplan led the attack: [David Campbell has] *demonstrated a pattern of activity...that the welfare of the department itself, the welfare of the university, the confidentiality of his colleagues, have all been placed in jeopardy by the frequent recanting of decisions. Secondly, he has become a recluse within the department. Third, there have been ethical questions recently raised about his own behavior.... His question of unethical behavior extends even to the basis of possible fraud with regard to the federal government in his own research efforts."* [Author's note: No charges of fraud by any party were ever made against David Campbell.]

Kaplan noted that Campbell had raised questions with residents, fellows, and local and national ophthalmologists, and that he was a "self-fulfilling prophet of doom" regarding the newspaper article.

In regard to Allen Gammon, the transcript shows that Kaplan accused Gammon of antagonizing many people within the department and pushing his secretary to open other doctors' mail and spy on them to the point that she quit. Dr. Kaplan recalled Gammon's threat at the meeting hosted by Garland Perdue in March that Dr. Gammon would sue Dwight Cavanagh if he did not receive tenure. On this day, the committee heard only good things about Cavanagh's behavior and bad things about Gammon and Campbell. Cavanagh's inner circle had scored points for their chairman.

* * *

AUGUST 8, 1985—THURSDAY

At 6:30 PM promptly, after a long day in the clinic, Dr. David Campbell faced the Tindall Committee, Hunter Allen, Roy Townsend, and the court reporter. He looked down the long table and saw few friendly faces. His unease mounted, but he recalled the words of his personal lawyer two days earlier. His lawyer reported a conversation with Hunter Allen, who had said it was not necessary for Campbell to have his own lawyer present. They were going to ask him questions about Dwight Cavanagh, not David Campbell. Comforted by this reassurance, Campbell ignored the small voice in his gut that urged him to turn around and walk out.

George Tindall welcomed him, confirming that the investigation was about Cavanagh, and never mentioned the fact that Campbell himself was the subject of inquiry as well.

Campbell first recounted the worries of Robert Allen (Campbell's glaucoma partner who had resigned from the faculty) and Allen's anguish over the undiagnosed, blind glaucoma patients. Campbell, diffident and tentative, offered indirect answers when pressed about his concerns.

When asked if he felt that Cavanagh had overbilled his patients, Campbell replied, *The specifics were that Dr. Cavanagh had dictated, as I recall—and again, Dr. Waring can probably do a better job with this than I can—had dictated that he had done a certain operation called a membranectomy. The question came up, had membranectomies been done…. My feeling was that—once again, my vote said that I did not know for sure that this had occurred but that I wasn't completely clear in my heart that it had not occurred.*

On his feelings about Cavanagh at the conclusion of the Waring Committee proceedings, Campbell said, *My position at that point was that the possible harmful care to patients had now stopped and the school had been notified, which I felt to be appropriate and, finally, I felt that we had to look for a change in Dwight's character so that this behavior would not occur again, but that I was happy at that point with what had happened.*

Campbell was then asked, *What kind of change in character?*

He replied, *Well, just something so that, if these causes of concern that we had were true, that things like that would not happen again.*

Campbell was then asked if he told Hatcher that Dwight's head should be "on a platter."

He said, *I would deny that…. People have asked me this time around if I feel that—what I feel should be done. First of all, I'd like to say that it's not my position to say what should be done. But I would like to state that in this context, if these matters all turn out to be true, then I think it's—and I vacillate on this. It's possible that someone might say this is inappropriate behavior for a chairman. But on the other hand, I then go—I vacillate and I say we've got to look at other factors. And it's basically not my decision, but I never said anything like "head on a platter."*

On some issues Dr. Campbell was clear and direct. He had never talked to the press, Houston's family, or Houston's lawyer. He wanted an unbiased group to judge Cavanagh's behavior, and Campbell would abide by their decision.

As the meeting progressed, even though Tindall had not informed Campbell that the committee was charged with judging his own behavior as well as Cavanagh's, Campbell began to realize this was not just about Cavanagh. Even so, he ached to hear the opinion of outside, respected faculty. After four hours, Campbell walked out into the humid August night with the growing knowledge that the decisions of this committee could affect his career as well as Dwight Cavanagh's.

* * *

AUGUST 10, 1985—SATURDAY

The Tindall Committee devoted most of the day to hearing from three witnesses: Ms. Frankie Stegall and Drs. Allen Gammon and Dwight Cavanagh. Ms. Stegall led off with a litany of complaints about Dr. Gammon and generally agreed with previous testimony about the timing of events. The committee learned nothing new from her.

Allen Gammon entered the room in the middle of the morning. Noting Hunter Allen's presence, Gammon went on the offensive. He said, *Before you start, as you know, we'd discussed on at least two occasions who was on the committee, and you hadn't told me that there would be attorneys here, that there would be counsel here, and I'd like to know why that is.*

Tindall said, *You asked me for the names of the committee, and I freely gave you the names of the members of the committee. Mr. Allen is here because he is the representative of the clinic. There is litigation that has been filed.*

Gammon asked, *So you're saying that he represents me?*

I'm saying that he represents the entire clinic.

But if these are legal proceedings, then I believe that I would have the right to counsel, myself.

Tindall stammered, *These are not—this is a hearing in which we would like to ask you questions. It is not...*

If that's the case, then I don't see the requirement for counsel.

I do, said Tindall.

Well, we'll have to disagree on that issue.

All right. I take it, then, that you are not willing to appear before us?

Is that what I said, George?

Can we begin asking you questions?

I'm here of my own free will. I offered to come. I'm just saying at the outset, you know, you walk into an operating room and everybody is gloved except one person, if you care about what you're doing, you point that out. If you're not serious about what you're doing, then maybe it doesn't matter.

Okay.

I'm serious about why I'm here. I care about the patients. I care about the clinic. I care about the truth.

Gammon's direct, combative tone continued throughout. He recounted the child whose eye was lost to infection because of Cavanagh's neglect and unaccountable delay in surgery. He made it clear that the Waring Committee's review was neither appropriate nor thorough: *The facts don't fit the findings, and the findings don't fit the recommendations.* He noted that employees can't judge their boss when salaries, space, promotions, and reputations can be affected.

Gammon said that the Waring Committee should have interviewed both Philip Newman and Genevieve Switz, especially since Newman had told Gammon that Cavanagh had altered Houston's chart. He further said, *Bob Allen needs to be talked to by anybody that wants to know the truth in these matters.*

One of the committee members specifically asked him, *You're charging that they did not interview anyone in the operating room— anesthesiologists, nurses, Dr. Newman, or anyone—involved with this case except Dr. Cavanagh?*

That's my understanding.

Another asked Gammon, *What do you think about Dr. Cavanagh's ability to govern the department and section given all this that's gone on? Can he be effective, do you think?*

Gammon said, *He has told me and others that he was sick, and I think it depends on whether that is correctable, and whether, if not correctable, it's controlled. I do not...*

Sick with what?

His word to me was *"had become irrational."* His word to others was *"impaired physician." Everybody has a label. I don't know what the appropriate label is. I'm not sure it matters.*

The meeting meandered along, and no other questions were asked concerning Cavanagh's ability to remain chairman. Tindall called a lunch break while Gammon was pointing out other deficiencies in the Waring Committee's work. After lunch, Gammon was gone.

Gammon had clearly stated the need for a more thorough investigation than the Waring Committee had performed. In Gammon's opinion, the Tindall Committee had a lot of work left to do.

After lunch the committee spent the rest of the afternoon with Dwight Cavanagh, who had interrupted his beach vacation for this hearing.

After formally informing Cavanagh that the committee's job was to investigate the Houston surgery and Cavanagh's performance, Tindall invited Cavanagh to tell them about Houston's surgery.

Cavanagh began: *That occurred in September of 1983...and I had been here since 1976. That's seven, just about seven years to the day. And during that period of time, since I came, the section had gone from 1389 patients in 1976 to this year about 35,000 so that by 1983...I don't remember what we were up to, but it was in the twenties of thousands. And during that period of time, I just had become increasingly pulled in about six different directions.*

I was charged with the responsibility of developing an eye center and funding it. Some of you may not know that there is not a dime of your money in that building on our side. All of the money for the ophthalmology side was raised.

The second thing I was charged with was building up the department.... So we recruited some fifteen people over that seven-year period....

The second [sic] *thing was to get the research effort up to snuff; and when I took over, I think we had about $50,000 worth of grants, and this last year, we've had about $2 million. So to accomplish that, I was a clinician, surgeon, fund-raiser, department chairman,* *and I went to NIH and got on every influential committee I could get on....*

Now during that period of time—I make no apology to you gentlemen—I made some mistakes. I just got myself spread out to the point where I didn't know, you know, which end was up sometimes. And during that period of time, I feel quite certain that I did some things that I ought not to have done, and I left undone some things I should have done. But I did the best I could....

Now, the Sargus Houston affair started back in May or so.... He had one good eye. He had disease in both eyes, cataract and lattice dystrophy. One eye was still good, about 20/25, 20/30, somewhere in there.

So I came back from vacation, and he was in the hospital. The first thing we found out was that all our nurses had quit....

So, between that state of mind, that situation, and an inept fellow, and the final straw was that his surgery was delayed....

And then I was called into a meeting in Dr. Hatcher's office that afternoon.... And the substance of the meeting was, Dr. Brumbley felt that my chief fund-raiser, Mr. Wayne,...he felt that he should be let go.... Now without Mr. Wayne, no money; without money, no department....

So I walked out of that office like that, and I walked over to the operating room. And it could have been one of you there and nobody...we just didn't check....

I walked in the operating room.... I said, "Is the patient blocked? Block the patient." The PA blocked the patient, with Anesthesia standing there, giving him Valium IV, in the wrong eye. And we proceeded to operate on the wrong eye.

Things went well. I turned to him and said, "do you want to close?" He said, "Fine." So I left the room and went out.

At that point, I was sitting out there dictating all my operative notes for the day.... Well, about that time, Anesthesia came in, and I believe it was Berry, and said, you know "It says on the chart we're supposed to operate on the right eye." It was obvious we operated on the wrong eye.

So I called the patient's sister.... I told her that we had inadvertently operated on the wrong eye. I didn't say we made a mistake, we blew it. I said, "We did not operate on the eye we intended to," my exact words. And I'm almost certain to her, in thinking about it, that I used the word "inadvertently." But I didn't say, "Gosh, we just made the world's greatest error. We blew it." I said, "We didn't operate on the eye we intended to. I think it's going to be all right. The surgery went well."

And Monday night, we called a faculty meeting, and I said I only wanted the doctors there.... I told them that night that I didn't blame anybody, that if the captain ran the aircraft carrier on...if the lieutenant ran the aircraft carrier on the rocks coming into San Diego while the captain was in the engine room, it was the captain's responsibility, and I wasn't blaming anybody for it. It was my responsibility, that whole damn thing. And then after that, we took the best care of the old man we could.

The last time I saw him was in September of 1984. I asked him if he wanted his glasses changed. He says, "No, Doc." He says, "I'm doing real well." He put on his brown hat with the bandana around it and walked out in the hall, and that was the last time I saw him.

I don't think there's a person in the clinic, in the operating room, in the department, or in the state of Georgia that within two weeks didn't know that Cavanagh had operated on the wrong eye.

At that, three members of the committee promptly said they had no idea of the wrong-eye surgery until this series of meetings began a few days ago.

Cavanagh resumed and answered whether he had told the PA specifically which eye to block or just to block the patient.

I didn't tell her which eye to block. I told her to block the eye. There's no reason to tell her which eye.... There are about eighteen things in an operating room which makes that not happen [blocking the wrong eye]. One, you come in, the nurse asks you which eye you are there for. The second thing, if the block occurs in the room, which it sometimes does, the nurse, Anesthesia, and everyone always asks the patient which eye are you there for.

Bear in mind, this man is awake. It's local. And bear in mind the nurse came in, and the one who started the case stopped and left, and then another one came in and picked up, and she didn't know. The PA and Anesthesia stood there without looking at the chart. I mean, it's my responsibility not to have picked it up, but I would say that every fail-safe mechanism in an operating room that exists failed.

The questions went on and on, shifting from Houston to the Waring Committee. Cavanagh's reaction to the committee was: *I was pretty hurt, and I was pretty shaken up, and I basically am a gentleman and try to believe the best of the world. I have learned differently since then.... I was very angry at Waring for a while; but I think in retrospect, I have come to believe that he did what he thought was the right thing to do, and he did it well.*

Dr. Cavanagh explained the overbilling for membranectomy in patients who had keratoconus, where no membrane existed: *Now, I also do that in keratoconus cases, but I'm not excising a retro-corneal fibrous membrane. I'm doing a retrocorneal bevel. Many of the times when I get going on my operative notes and I'm sitting there—and I've become careful since then to call it beveling instead of retrocorneal dissection. You get going on those op notes, and you say "retrocorneal dissection," and the words "fibrous membrane" just come. I mean, it's just stupid. It's just stupid. And it's like—I mean, God almighty, if somebody was charged that shouldn't have been, fine. But it's a $40 mistake on a $2500 operation. Plus, if I wanted to, I could have billed them half again for the vitrectomy, which I have never done, which would have added another $1500 to the operation, and Medicare would have paid it.* [Author's note: The extra charge for membranectomy in keratoconus cases that had no membrane was $140 ($308 in 2008), and in such keratoconus cases, vitrectomy is not performed and should not have been charged under any circumstance.]

Is Cavanagh still able to run his department?

The thing is, I try to be a democrat. I have always tried to have the kind of group where we make group decisions and group process, and that's a very painful way to run a department.

Is the faculty satisfied that the issue is closed, Campbell and Gammon excepted?

Cavanagh: *I'm absolutely positive they are. I'll tell you why, because we've been through it four times. We reopened this—this is about the fourth time around.*

Now, we put this issue to bed. The whole faculty met. The committee went through the report, and how they had done it in October and November. It was over, except throughout the whole American Academy of Ophthalmology meeting in Atlanta here, there it was all over again. There was a cover-up. He should have been thrown out and wasn't. He's been replaced as chairman. I mean, the rumors are out. Somebody was talking. Somebody was talking. That died down.

Just before the dedication, the suit came out.... After being quiet for two months—I didn't know Campbell was doing anything. All of a sudden, people were beginning to say, "Dwight, Campbell is at it again. He's just not letting go. He's just after this thing." I said, "What are you talking about?" And he said he was going behind closed doors, talking to everybody; and he's saying that everyone— that this time his tact was, oh everyone is so unhappy. It was unhappiness. I am unhappy; you're unhappy...unhappy, unhappy.

So we held two meetings.... And I mean, at the end of the second night, they all voted 100%. Then they inscribed a plaque to me, and Campbell signed it and so did Gammon....

The next thing that happened was, in early May, at the Georgia Eye Society meeting at the Cloister, Campbell comes up to me and says that at the cocktail party on Saturday night, he says, "Gammon is pushing buttons. He's going to push the nuclear button."

Five minutes later the president of the MAG [sic] *comes up and said, "Do you know the little guy just came up and said do I know how he can make a complaint to the Ethics Committee?"*

Dr. Gammon, unfortunately, sometimes has been a little bit loose with the truth; and he's been known to do this on a number of occasions....

The question shifted to the issue of Cavanagh making derogatory remarks about other Georgia doctors in his referral letters. Hunter Allen quoted a letter Cavanagh had written discussing a particular patient: *I understand that he saw young Dave Henderson* [name changed]. *I like Dave as a person. He certainly is not very dynamic, however. And every patient that I have ever seen who has seen him has expressed great fear about his surgical abilities.*

To which Cavanagh admitted, *Which is true but probably shouldn't have been said.*

The afternoon dragged on, and Cavanagh's answers became longer and longer. One member asked, *What do you think of the future of Gammon and Campbell in your department?*

Without hesitation, Cavanagh answered, *The moving finger writes and having writ moves on. Nor all your piety nor wit shall lure it back to cancel half a line, nor all your tears wash out a word of it.*

There is a point in time where a man crosses the river in a relationship. Relationships are alive. They can die. And we have a dead relationship, between not only myself, but I think just about everybody in that building over there and those two individuals. Basic trust has been violated. I mean, it just isn't there.

Cavanagh continued until Tindall interrupted him for his final thoughts on the two. Cavanagh replied, *George, these people need to be divorced, period. You can't afford not to. I mean, first, it is the right thing to do. You have to do the right thing. And this is the right thing. They have to go.*

Now you know, are they going to try to blackmail me? Well, if they try to blackmail me, fine. After it's on the front page of the

Sunday paper, I doubt seriously in my mind if...I mean, what are they going to do now, take out an ad?

The meeting and the day had almost ended, but the committee asked Cavanagh why Campbell had persisted in reopening the issues.

You know, I really lie awake thinking about this. I'll tell you what I think and how I feel. Bear in mind this is just my opinion, and I can be completely wrong.

Now, David has a history of problems with authority figures. And in Boston, the thing that ran him out was, he tried to take over the glaucoma service at the Mass. Eye and Ear Infirmary. He went to Dr. Chandler and Dr. Grant and asked their blessing to run off the part-time staff who were heads of it. You know, that was in some respects analogous to this present situation. I mean, it was just stupid, and he had to leave quickly. He came down. [Authors note: I interviewed Dr. Thomas Hutchinson, a respected senior Harvard faculty member, who told me there was no truth to these statements by Cavanagh. David Campbell was a well-respected and well-liked figure when he left Boston.]

He seemed to do well here. We did well for the first three or four years, and then he just became angry. It happened after 1981, I guess. Frank Bell and he and I were the ones that were here. Frank was a pure and simple clinician. He liked to operate, he liked to see patients, he liked to go home. And he never wrote a paper here in five, seven years. He never wrote one. I never encouraged him to leave. I told him there would always be a place for somebody that wanted to do that here, especially since the three of us kind of started the department together.

I think it was like one of those things where three young men after high school start a company and one of them ends up as president and the other two, instead of ending up somewhere, they're down and still at the bottom where they were. And Frank left in 1981. David became very angry. He felt left out of the power structure. I kept trying to include him administratively in every way I could, but he's not an administrator. He can't even administer his own section.

I think the practice issues, if you want my honest opinion, one can make a legitimate moral case for being appalled or upset or whatever, but I think that wasn't the real issue. I think the real issue was that I had to go....

[David had] *mixed issues. The thing that tells that to me most clearly it's a mixed issue, if the only issue is problem-solving of clinical problems and morality, if he was correct in what he told everybody, I* [Campbell] *just want the problem solved, then when the problem was solved, it would have been solved, but it wasn't. A week after he appended his signature to this* [faculty report supporting Cavanagh], *David asked Frankie Stegall to get Dr. Calhoun because she's known him for 20 years, to go to the university and take his name off the* [endowed] *chair* [held by Cavanagh]. *And then when she refuses to go, he goes and tries to himself, and the old man told him to go to hell.*

It's like Adler says in his hierarchy of dysfunctional goals, you know, attention-getting, acting out, attention-getting; but when you get down into revenge and inadequacy and you're in a blaming mechanism for dealing with the problems of the world, and you're emotionally centered to boot, which he is, then you've got a real problem in dealing with the mid-life crisis, which is what I think he's in. I am his mid-life crisis, and he isn't going to be happy until I'm dead. I can just tell you.

On Friday, he'll be at your feet. I'm so sorry, how can I get back on the team. I don't want to talk to Sargus Houston. And Monday he's in the dean's office. I mean, it's just—I don't know.

Gammon is not near as dangerous as he is. You all sat here and listened to him. He's very respectable. He's a nice guy. He's a decent person; and depending on what his mood is—I mean, he's told Meredith before, and I think Hunter was listening, all he wants to do is help me. Then he goes to Hatcher. He wants my head on a plate, that I'm not fit to work at a medical school around residents as a role model. I mean, I don't know; but I know he needs another job.

It is stupid to try to run a department if you're marching towards the German lines with your flags in your bayonets and the rest of the troops are in the trenches, refusing to follow you. You know, then it's a hopeless situation. That's not my sense of this matter at this point. It's bad that it happened; but in a way, it's like a goddamn pancreatic abscess. I mean, you can try to wall it off with antibiotics, but sometimes you've got to operate. I think what we're doing in the process is walling off with antibiotics, and I think it's time to operate on it.

Tindall asked him for his assurance that he would not go back to a hundred patients a day and ten operations, and Cavanagh replied, *I'll give you my assurances on that, George. I just feel burned to a crisp by this whole thing, not just the present episode. But I did that for eight years. I mean, it's just absolutely out-and-out amazing that something worse didn't happen.*

Tindall said, *Well, thank you, my friend. I appreciate your coming all the way off your vacation.* The committee trudged out of the littered room, tired, their weekend ruined, knowing that hours lay yet ahead of them. Cavanagh drove back to Hilton Head Island, his fate in the hands of this committee.

* * *

AUGUST 20, 1985

The Tindall Committee reconvened at 6:30 on a Tuesday evening. George Tindall welcomed Dr. Philip Newman.

After hearing Newman's version of the surgical proceedings on Sargus Houston, a member asked Newman the details of Cavanagh's postoperative discussion with Houston.

Newman said that on the day after the surgery, *Mr. Houston did ask at that point that he thought it was the other eye to be done;*

and, you know, Dwight said that he had intended to operate on both eyes and that he had changed his mind and decided to operate on the eye that was the left in this case instead of the right eye and that everything had gone well. That was pretty much the end of that, and Mr. Houston didn't say anything about anything. And we all left.

Later in the discussion, Hunter Allen pinned Newman down on the specific details by asking, *Was it your impression that your marching orders were that you were to perpetuate this belief that the left eye ultimately had been operated on because Dwight intended to operate on it?*

Dr. Newman replied, *That was the impression I had gotten.... Whenever Dwight does talk to family members, he always presents the positive side—that things went well. So I was just emulating that; and I said we operated on the left eye, that everything had gone well. I really didn't make much of a point that we had originally intended to operate on the right eye, that we had operated on the wrong eye; and, you know, I just left it as, you know, we operated on the left eye, and I knew that she* [Houston's sister] *was under the impression that we were going to be operating on the right eye, but that Dr. Cavanagh had decided to operate on the left eye, and that everything had gone well.*

Why did Newman fear consequences for himself? *Why do you think that because you were low man on the totem pole that you were going to be blamed for this? That seems unusual to me. What had happened in the past that gave you that sort of feeling that the blame would be passed down?*

Newman: *Well, nothing specifically ever happened to me that made me think that, you know, that the blame would be passed on to me. But, just some of—some of Dwight's, you know, people used to tell me stories about the way Dwight treated them, you know. Waring would tell me stories about how Dwight would talk about him out in the community, and Wilson would tell me stories about how Dwight would talk about him in the community.*

An hour or so later, Newman realized that the committee had never seen Sargus Houston's chart. After admitting to the changes he had made and unmade, he said, *Nobody has asked me about the other changes in the record. You know, there are changes in the actual history and physical sheet that nobody has asked me about. The orders are—the order changes I made, and I own up to that. But there are other changes in the order sheets which give different impressions of what was to be done at different times, and none of you all have asked me about that.*

Dr. Tindall said, *May I ask you to tell us about that?*

Another member joined in: *Tell us about it, because we haven't seen the records.*

Newman asked, *Do you have the records?*

Hunter Allen said, *Roy, they're down in your office. Do you want to go get them?*

As the group looked at the pages Newman had brought with him, the pages which had chart alterations of even the first visit the patient had made to Cavanagh, a member asked Newman, *Whose handwriting is that?*

Newman said, *Well, I mean—I can guess at whose handwriting it is, but I can't tell you for sure whose handwriting it is. To me, this looks like Dwight's handwriting. But if you want to—you know, there are questionable-document examiners who can tell whose handwriting this is....*

After even more discussion about Newman's impressions of the effects of the Houston surgery on the faculty, Tindall excused him with great appreciation for appearing before the group.

By now it was late, but the meeting's work was not done. They had one witness yet to interview—George Waring.

After welcoming Dr. Waring back from two weeks on the Colorado River, the committee began questioning him about his committee's work. Waring took pains here to point out that he did not perform a systematic investigation:

When I say our committee was a clinical investigation, if you please, as opposed to a systematic inquiry, we dealt with information that we had, and in some cases we tried to look a bit beyond. But we did not mount an external inquiry. We didn't call witnesses. We didn't go on to systematically review one year of charts or something like that.

We did not make an attempt, and I'll emphasize again our committee was really not an investigative committee...we were a review committee, and I think the distinction is very important. We did not set out as an investigative group to get to the bottom of things. We set out as a review group to try to see what was going on, where were the problems, identify them, and then deal with them in a way which we felt appropriate, which was, A, confronting Dwight with them systematically and, B, passing them on to our superiors in the clinic and university.

Waring did point out that the only systematic review was of all the patients with Fuchs' dystrophy within one year. One committee member asked him, *The one area where you did do that was when you reviewed the slides for one year, and how many did you find that you did not agree with the clinical diagnosis?*

Waring said, *The numbers are very fuzzy in my mind. We reviewed the cases, the cases of Fuchs' dystrophy, if I'm going to guess, were probably fifty; and I'm going to guess we found five or six cases that didn't fit. It may not be accurate, but that's the ballpark.*

Another member asked, *In dealing with the entity, would ten percent error like that be considered exorbitant?*

Waring said, *It would be considered unacceptable.*

George Tindall asked Waring about David Campbell. Waring replied, *Well, I believe that David—and I'm expressing this as my personal opinion only—is a man of great integrity and a man who is truly bothered by the events that you reviewed....*

Second is that David is not alone in the department. I wish to emphasize that. We are truly a spectrum. We may be a little bit more a camp, like right now; that David is not standing somehow as a wild man in the wilderness by himself. There are other department members who are concerned about, A, these things that were done, still of concern to them, and, B, Dwight's political method of dealing with people; is it fair, is it aboveboard, is it honest, is it straightforward, is it supportive, is it good?

George Tindall then asked, *Can I follow? Is he a good role model?*

Waring glanced over at the court reporter, shifted in his seat, and looked back at Tindall. He said, *I'll be glad to discuss these things if she would quit typing.*

I don't think he's as good a role model as that I would like to see. And if you all...and I can maybe say, most clear to say, I think Dwight is primarily a politician. And I think that his main calling in life is political. I think his main interest in life is political. In that sense, I'm not sure that it is a very good role model. I don't think the quality of care that we reviewed is a good role model, trying to do three times as much. And as a scientist, I think if Dwight took the time, I think he could be a good role model. God knows, he has the training for it. He's certainly smart enough. But, again, his major emphasis has really been political, not scientific, even though he is fostering a scientific institution.

I think that this is, maybe, some of the...you asked me what's wrong in the department, and I'm glad to follow that with a question of mistrust. There is mistrust among some of us. Many people don't trust Dwight, as he has, shall I call it, a political approach to dealing with people as opposed to maybe an absolutely sincere approach, although he would tell you he is absolutely sincere. I know how he feels about it. One of the problems in our department is mistrust....

Another member asked, *Is there another emotion going on in the department? Is fear present in the department or concern for position of people in the department?*

Yes.

Is there a fear of Dwight's retaliation?

Yes. Dwight is—and here, I keep trying to define by politician.... And we have a political department in that sense. I think that breeds some mistrust, some fear, a bit of divisiveness.

Is he a good surgeon?

The answer is yes, he is a technically acceptable surgeon. Now, he's not interested in what I might call meticulous aspects of surgical technique. He is interested in getting done. But he is not a clumsy, ham-handed surgeon....

After a few more questions and concluding remarks, the group scattered into the darkness. Other sessions lay ahead, then some hard decisions.

* * *

AUGUST 22, 1985—THURSDAY

The Tindall Committee convened at 6:30 PM to hear only one witness, Dr. William Coles. He had come to Atlanta from Charleston, bringing not only his expertise in ophthalmology, but a business in antique furniture as well. Unhappy with events, he was actively seeking a chairmanship in other Departments of Ophthalmology.

Coles explained why he had met with Tindall and now this committee: *I came to George* [Tindall], *and after a time of feeling that there was...you are seeing a lot of polarization in the department and actually talking to people that had a great deal of interest in and a great deal of, I don't know, emotion in the areas that they're talking about. I came to George and said "I wanted you to know that there are members of the department that are pretty much in the middle of the road...."*

Those of us that tried to stay in the middle ground were, indeed, distressed by what we found as a committee in reviewing the clinical practice.... At the time that the committee ended its deliberations, there were a number of us that were amazed at what we found. We felt that there was a degree of clinical practice here that we were totally unaware of, and we were somewhat shocked by that.

We were living with knowledge that there had been, we felt, a sort of substandard of practice. And I am not particularly talking about a single case. I am not talking about a mistake; I'm talking about a standard of practice that we were concerned about.

A committee member asked Coles what he thought of Cavanagh's abilities as department chairman.

I don't think there's any secret that I'm trying actively to leave the department.... I think one of the reasons that I really am leaving is that I disagree with some of Dwight's management capabilities... yet I wouldn't want you to go away without knowing my impression, that I think the problems that we are in at this time are generated because of Dwight's personality. All the positives and intellectual capabilities, the leadership qualities that he handles in certain places, I do believe that he's had a responsibility for the polarization that we see at this time....

Another member asked: *Do you feel that the problems that he had in the past are so serious and so unacceptable that he can no longer lead the section in the clinic effectively? In other words, with the history that he has, can he be the kind of role model that the clinical side of the department needs to go forward?"*

Coles answered, *I think it's going to be extremely difficult for him to act as a role model for residents and students over the next four to five years; I would think I don't think that's going to be easy for him.*

The questions went on and on. The committee wanted to know what Coles would do to straighten out the department from here on. Coles pointed out that the Tindall Committee was very important in the healing process, that an independent examination of the issues and report would help the department. Further, *most of us will respond to the decisions that are made in this committee. The way that you have done it, with the thoroughness that you have done it, that will help us very much.*

What about patient care?

I think the standard of patient care is very, very high. I think... for example, I think David Campbell probably is one of the most honest physicians I've ever known. I think he's one of the most honest researchers I have ever known. That's one of the reasons I would hate to see him leave this department. He adds a great, great deal to this department.

Bob Smith, a surgeon on the committee, took the question even further. *But how do you explain the fact that an ophthalmologist with Dwight's obvious skill and information would operate on someone with a diagnosis of Fuchs' dystrophy who didn't have it? How do you explain that he would operate on someone with a diagnosis that didn't exist?*

Coles shifted in his chair. *I can't explain that. I think it's one of the things that has bothered us most, is that some of the things that happen seem not to be directly related to being overworked. They seem to be in a sense a lack of care for the patient, and it's one of the hardest things to deal with. I don't know.*

I mean, I can understand maybe one case that would come out, but there seemed to be a pattern as we were reviewing those cases that many of us were concerned....

Smith interrupted, *Maybe let me ask it a different way. If you took everybody in your department and went through their practice with the same degree of care that apparently has been given to Dwight's practice during that same period of time, and admittedly didn't review every patient, but they certainly turned up a lot of discrepancies, would you expect to see anything like that degree of discrepancy in your practice or Waring's? I mean, we're all human, we're going to make some errors, but we're talking about a substantial number, perhaps, in Dwight's practice. If you went through your other department chairman or other department members, would you see anything like that?"*

Coles shot back, *No, no.*

You don't hesitate a minute to say that?

Not at all. I think it's one of the hardest things we've had to deal with...and I do not believe that if we went through George Waring's practice, a corneal surgeon, if we went through Lou Wilson's practice, a corneal surgeon, that we would find this. I don't believe it's just an overworked problem at all. I do not believe it.

After three hours, the session ended. Dr. Tindall noted that another "middle-of-the-road" faculty member, Robert Spector, wanted to address the committee, but that Tindall felt nothing new would be gained. Tindall obtained the committee's approval to interview Dr. Spector by telephone. Coles was the last witness formally interviewed by the committee. The court reporter, Hunter Allen, Roy Townsend, and Garland Perdue were excused.

Now the work began. Only a limited number of people were interviewed, and Houston's chart had remained out of the room until Newman offered to show the chart changes made by someone other than himself. Genevieve Switz, John Wright, Bob Allen, Houston's family, and numerous other individuals who could offer testimony damning to Cavanagh were never heard from. Yet, unsettling things had been said and recorded.

What would the Tindall Committee do? Would the words of Cavanagh's allies prevail, the first and carefully orchestrated performance that supported Cavanagh and condemned Campbell? Or would the last witness, Bill Coles, prevail? Would his more neutral testimony with strong support for Campbell's character and major concerns about Cavanagh's practice pattern sway the committee?

Would it register with the committee that Dr. Waring felt his committee's work to be a review at best and not a full-fledged investigation? Would the committee read between the lines and hear Waring's plea for a full investigation? Would Dr. Newman's recommendation to employ a handwriting expert be followed? Would the committee decide it needed to interview more people or employ experts to help them determine the truth of the events that had occurred?

This committee had the power to exonerate or ruin the careers of three well-known academic ophthalmologists with national reputations. It devoted four more hours to meetings, from 6:30 to 9:00 PM on August 26 and from 6:30 to 8:15 PM on August 29.

Tindall signed the committee report on September 5, and the last member affixed his signature on September 10. In the interim, on September 9, the most important committee of the Emory Clinic, the Administrative Committee, met to consider Tindall's report. Chaired by Garland Perdue, the Administrative Committee comprised all the section heads, department chairs, the dean of the School of Medicine, and the vice president and director of the Woodruff Health Sciences Center.

The report itself was quite lengthy, with a preamble of five single-spaced pages. The preamble concluded with specific statements about the activities of Campbell and Gammon:

Despite the fact that all members of the Ophthalmology Department met at length to investigate and discuss the issue, and despite the fact that responsible university officials (e.g., Drs. Hatcher and Perdue) were satisfied that a thorough investigation had been performed and that appropriate actions were taken, Drs. David Campbell and Allen Gammon made allegations that the investigation was not done in a proper manner and that all the facts have not been brought to light, etc. Dr. Campbell has been the more vocal of the two. There is ample evidence that Dr. Campbell has persisted in making the statements and allegations and has taken the issue to many people in responsible positions including Drs. Perdue, Hatcher, Warren, Laney, as well as ophthalmologists in the Atlanta area and other cities and institutions. The essence of the concerns and allegations is that the institution is covering up facts of the Cavanagh investigation. In persisting with these allegations to a large number and variety of people, Dr. Campbell has implicated the entire Emory Clinic in the alleged wrongdoings and cover-ups, which he claims exist in the Department of Ophthalmology....

We have also heard testimony from all of the people listed above, and questions related to all of the above issues were asked of each individual who came before our committee.

Our conclusions and recommendations follow:
1. *Was the original investigation (internal committee of the Department of Ophthalmology) adequate and correct?*
Our committee concludes that the investigation was not only adequate and correct but very thorough.

2. *Should the investigation be reopened?*
Our committee concludes that it should not be reopened.

3. *Were the actions taken by the clinic director responsible and correct?*
Our committee feels that Dr. Perdue took all steps possible to resolve this issue, including holding lengthy meetings with the entire ophthalmology faculty on more than one occasion. Our committee concludes that Dr. Perdue acted responsibly and correctly.

4. *Is there evidence of current impropriety in the section of ophthalmology?*
We've found no evidence of **current** *[emphasis added] impropriety in the section of ophthalmology.*

5. *Is Dr. Cavanagh, the section head, fit to continue in office?*

The committee concludes that prior to 1984 there were deficiencies in Dr. Cavanagh's medical practice. These were primarily due to extenuating circumstances, most notably Dr. Cavanagh's overloaded academic, administrative, and clinical responsibilities...our committee feels that these heavy responsibilities had an adverse effect upon Dr. Cavanagh's practice to the extent that, at times, the standards of medical care and his judgment in some cases were not up to that expected of the clinic partner.

In view of the many academic and administrative duties with which Dr. Cavanagh is charged, our committee recommends:

1. *That the Department of Ophthalmology shall be restructured in such a way that will allow Dr. Cavanagh to designate a member of the Ophthalmology Department to serve as deputy section head and charge this individual with the responsibility of managing the clinic section.*
2. *That Dr. Cavanagh continue to restrict his medical practice to a relatively small number of patients.*
3. *That his medical and surgical practice of ophthalmology be monitored as is currently being done for at least another 12 months.*

The Administrative Committee accepted these recommendations as well as those concerning David Campbell and Allen Gammon. The committee recommended a formal reprimand of David Campbell and no action for Allen Gammon.

On this same day, David Campbell placed a phone call to Louis Wilson. Campbell had been unable to locate Dwight Cavanagh, so he gave Wilson the message. Campbell was resigning, by phone this moment and in writing in a letter coming soon. Campbell had realized over his summer vacation that he could no longer remain at Emory. He had been contemplating this for months, and the Tindall Committee had forced a decision. He wanted to stay for the remainder of the academic year and depart in about nine months.

* * *

On the next day, Tuesday, September 10, after the last two doctors signed the Tindall Report, Emory officials chose to make public the results of this putative confidential peer-review process. Their decision to go public would lead to a swirl of legal decisions in the years ahead.

* * *

NEWS

Woodruff Medical Center Information Office
Emory University 1440 Clifton Rd, NE
Atlanta, Georgia
Release Date: September 10, 1985 Sylvia Wrobel
Information Officer
Subject: STANDARDS & ETHICS COMMITTEE PRESENTS
REPORT

The Professional Standards and Ethics Committee of the Emory Clinic reported Monday afternoon, September 9, that it had conducted extensive rehearings of all concerns and allegations expressed with regard to the Section of Ophthalmology of the Emory Clinic and specifically with regard to Dr. Dwight Cavanagh.

The committee, composed of tenured faculty members of the Emory University School of Medicine, concluded that two previous investigations were "adequate, correct, and very thorough," and recommended that the matter should be considered closed.

The report and its conclusions and recommendations were presented to, and unanimously accepted by, the Administrative Committee of the Emory Clinic at the September 9 meeting. Dr. Garland Perdue, director of the Emory Clinic, stated that he considers the action final. Dr. Cavanagh will continue in his present positions, according to Dr. Perdue.

The major conclusions reported by the Professional Standards and Ethics Committee are:

1. *There **has not ever been** [emphasis added], nor is there now, any "impropriety" in Dr. Cavanagh's practice.*

2. *Any difficulties encountered in Dr. Cavanagh's practice prior to 1984 were related to the combination of a large clinical practice and other heavy responsibilities, a combination which may have diminished the time he was able to spend with individual patients. These responsibilities included the development and funding of a major eye center, the recruitment of an outstanding faculty (from four to the current level of fifteen), the development and enhancement of research activities, and the acceptance of important roles in national organizations of ophthalmic surgeons and the National Institutes of Health.*

3. *The committee reviewed a 1983 case in which Dr. Cavanagh inadvertently operated on the incorrect eye of a patient. There was "no individual wrongdoing," the committee said, and the case was an isolated incident caused by his heavy workload.*

4. *The committee considered it "important to point out that the problems related to Dr. Cavanagh's practice have been and remain completely corrected, following Dr. Cavanagh's voluntary reduction of clinical responsibilities." Furthermore, Dr. Cavanagh's practice for the past year has been monitored, and all surgery has been found to be entirely necessary and well performed. In addition, Dr. Cavanagh has appointed a deputy section chief to assist him in management of clinical affairs.*

The information office rushed the release to Charles Seabrook of the *Atlanta Journal-Constitution* and to the public. Prior to his August article, Seabrook had interviewed Cavanagh in person. They met in Cavanagh's home. Only Seabrook and Cavanagh were present. Seabrook recalled that Cavanagh was quite agitated and disturbed, especially at the thought that his daughter would be reading unfavorable publicity. He told Seabrook that the people making these accusations would have to "meet their maker" someday.

With the Emory press release in hand, Seabrook telephoned Cavanagh for some additional quotes and wrote the following in the next day's *Atlanta Journal- Constitution*:

Wednesday, September 11, 1985

Emory review finds no "impropriety" in Cavanagh case

by Charles Seabrook
science/medicine writer

> *Emory University medical school officials said Tuesday that a heavy patient load and too many administrative duties apparently contributed to a patient having the wrong eye operated on by the chairman of the institution's Ophthalmology Department.*
>
> *That is one of the main findings of a two-month investigation by Emory's Professional Standards and Ethics Committee, which looked at a number of allegations against Dr. H. Dwight Cavanagh.*
>
> *The report said Cavanagh had not committed "any impropriety."*
>
> *Cavanagh said Tuesday that he was "very grateful and gratified by the outcome" of the investigation.*
>
> *Cavanagh is portrayed by the latest report as a brilliant surgeon, who was faced with an overwhelming administrative load while trying to carry on a full-time clinical practice....*
>
> *The statement Tuesday did say, however, that "an isolated" 1983 case in which Cavanagh operated on the wrong eye of an elderly patient was due to the eye doctor's heavy workload.*

An elderly Macon man, Sargus Houston, contends in a suit filed in Fulton Superior Court that Cavanagh performed surgery in the left eye when it should have been in the right. Houston says in the suit that he suffered permanent loss of vision because of the mistake.

Houston also claims in the suit that Cavanagh said the surgery had gone well.

In addition, the lawsuit charges that Cavanagh and some of his staff members altered the patient's medical record in an effort to conceal the negligence.

Cavanagh has admitted in court documents that he operated on the wrong eye, but he denies any attempt to cover it up. He has said in interviews that he is the victim of professional jealousy within his department....

But the latest investigation found that "there has not been, nor is there now, any impropriety on the part of Dr. Cavanagh."

Perdue said Tuesday that he considers his action and the report from the committee to be the final word on the subject.

Perdue had thought his meeting with the faculty in March had closed the matter. He was wrong then. Would this report indeed be the final word on the Cavanagh matter?

CHAPTER SEVEN

REVENGE

SEPTEMBER 1985

Charles Seabrook had been the first to receive anonymous phone calls, but he wasn't the only one. Sargus Houston's attorney Taylor Jones had heard early on from several unhappy Emory people as he began to put together his case. The most helpful was someone he never met, at least not knowingly.

"I want to be known as Dr. Z," the voice said. Jones didn't need to know his name, but he was in Emory's eye department. He had names and addresses of unhappy patients and a copy of the Waring Committee report. Jones needed to know there were many more blind patients than Sargus Houston; there was unnecessary surgery, fraud, and possible racism. Was Taylor Jones interested?

A delighted Taylor Jones would read material which was never supposed to leave the committee room. Now, how could he get this into evidence? He knew Hunter Allen would fight him at every level, claiming the sanctity of peer review.

* * *

Campbell's letter of resignation, dated September 16, 1985, one week after his conversation with Wilson, soon reached the desks of Cavanagh, Wilson, Meredith, and Perdue. Although Campbell received polite letters acknowledging his plans to stay until the fall of 1986 and thanking him for his service, the real reaction had to be unmitigated joy. The conscience of the department was leaving, and Cavanagh's team was fully in charge.

Dwight Cavanagh wasted no time sending a letter out to department chairs and friends around the country, celebrating his exoneration. After the usual pleasantries appropriate to the recipient, the letter went on:

With the deepest personal gratitude, I should like to acknowledge my appreciation for your expression of support and concern during recent events.... As you are aware, the university committee charged with resolving this matter has unanimously cleared me of any improprieties. One of the individuals involved in continued furtherance of these issues has been formally reprimanded for inappropriate actions and has submitted his resignation from the university.

Character, as the Greeks say, is fate. During this difficult time, I have tried to meet this challenge with the requisite courage and dignity required. With malice toward none, it has proven to be an opportunity for greater personal and spiritual growth; I believe we will go from strength to strength in the years ahead.

Thank you again for caring and reaching out at this time.

With grateful appreciation,

Dwight
H. Dwight Cavanagh, M.D., Ph.D.
The F. Phinizy Calhoun, Sr., M.D. Professor
Chairman, Department of Ophthalmology
Director, Emory Eye Center

Cavanagh included a copy of Seabrook's article and the news release from Emory. He didn't need to mention David Campbell's name. The grapevine took care of that detail.

While Dr. Cavanagh was bashing Campbell and Gammon around the country, the Administrative Committee humiliated Campbell on campus. Dr. Garland Perdue attended the ophthalmology faculty meeting in mid-September. Perdue commanded Campbell to stand in front of the faculty. Perdue then read the following letter, dated September 17, 1985:

PERSONAL AND CONFIDENTIAL
FOR YOUR EYES ONLY

Dear Dr. Campbell,

You are already aware of the content of the report of the Professional Standards and Ethics Committee of the Emory Clinic. You are aware that this committee is composed of persons of probity, experience, and wisdom. You are aware that their unanimous report was accepted and adopted by the unanimous vote of the Administrative Committee of the Emory Clinic. You are aware that this committee includes section heads and department chairman, the dean of the School of Medicine, and the vice president and director of the Woodruff Health Sciences Center.

It was the recommendation of the Professional Standards and Ethics Committee, unanimously approved by the Administrative Committee of the Emory Clinic, that you be reprimanded.

You are perceived to have asserted a moral superiority to your colleagues and peers, who had equal access to facts known to you and after evaluation arrived at different conclusions than you. You are perceived to have repudiated your colleagues and to have impugned the integrity of those charged with the duty of evaluating these facts, arriving at conclusions and recommendations and implementing action deemed to be appropriate.

You diminished your own credibility by alternate acceptance of conclusions and actions taken and subsequent recantation on at least two occasions. You carried on a program of questioning the actions of your colleagues before patients, employees and staff, and peers in the field of medicine. You are not likely so naive as to believe that conversing with multiple parties around the country could have any effect other than causing embarrassment and harm to your colleagues and your institution. You created disharmony and disruption and have caused incalculable damage to the prestige of your colleagues and your institution. You have expressed no shame or remorse, and you have offered no apology.

You are therefore reprimanded for your actions.

Garland D. Perdue, M.D.
Clinic Director

And so Emory University, owned by the Methodist Church, with a board partially comprised of Methodist bishops and headed by an ordained minister, reprimanded one of its faculty for asserting moral superiority.

* * *

OCTOBER 22, 1985

Dr. Louis Wilson met with Allen Gammon to discuss Gammon's fate. Gammon had wondered what was planned for him, and this was it: a precipitous move to Crawford Long in downtown Atlanta, Siberia in Emory terms, loss of his position as director of pediatric ophthalmology and strabismus at the Emory Clinic and as chief of ophthalmology at Emory's Egleston Hospital for Children. No halfway measures here; this was a total eradication of his presence at Emory.

Gammon had little recourse, but he did try to address the stated concerns of Cavanagh and his allies. On paper, the reason for the action was that acceptance of a recently awarded major grant would increase Gammon's research time to 70% of his "total effort," and he had to give something up to satisfy the rules of the National Eye Institute, the government agency awarding the grant. Gammon arranged for another researcher to take on 20% of the effort toward the grant and obtained approval from the NEI to continue practicing as he had before the grant. In a letter dated October 28, he argued that the grant was awarded because of the facilities on the Emory campus and that the NEI had approved of his reduced time on the grant. Reason and logic could not prevail against the real reason for his banishment. He never had a chance. Within a few days he was in downtown Atlanta with his wife as secretary, few resources, and no support. Mary Gemmill, previously Cavanagh's main technician, had to go as well, since she was the coordinator of the grant.

The club had cleaned house.

* * *

NOVEMBER 1985

Charles Seabrook pulled his grey pickup truck into the parking lot of Perimeter Mall, a shopping destination perched between Atlanta to the south and the affluent suburbs to the north. He could hear the constant roar of Atlanta's morning traffic on I-285. It was 8:00 AM, early for a reporter.

The calls about the Cavanagh case kept coming, despite the fervent wish of university officials that the Tindall Committee had settled the matter. Johnny Anonymous had called again, offering copies of the peer-protected reports if Seabrook would write his story as Johnny wanted to see it. Seabrook had refused.

Then a girl named Lisa had called, saying she was a former lover of one of the clinic attorneys and that she had information about the Cavanagh case. Would he meet her at 8:00 at Perimeter Mall? She would be driving a convertible. Seabrook patted the tape recorder in his pocket as a beautiful lady in her late twenties drove up, her dress hiked almost to her waist.

She told him to get in, that they would drive to a section of the parking lot to talk. Seabrook got in, trying to keep his eyes straight ahead, wondering what he had gotten himself into, hoping no one was watching.

She drove him over to a bench, and they both sat, not sure who would say what first.

She fumbled in her bag, asking permission to smoke, as Seabrook fumbled in his pocket, turning on his recorder. Georgia law allows tape-recording as long as one person consents; thus it is legal for anyone to tape his own conversation, even if the other party doesn't know about it. Seabrook later speculated to me that Lisa's fumbling was the attempt to activate her recorder just as he was doing the same with his.

She told Seabrook that she had been working in medical records at Emory for two years, that a lawyer had gotten her the job so she could keep a lookout for good cases. Well, she and the lawyer had split, and she was upset. What did Seabrook know about the Cavanagh case?

Whoa, thought Seabrook. *She's supposed to tell me stuff.* "Why don't you tell me what you know," he said.

She said she knew the wrong eye was operated on, and she knew the doctor tried to cover it up. As she went on, Seabrook realized that she was only telling him what anybody who read the newspaper would know. After a few more minutes, he figured it out: She was there to pump him for information. Somebody was worried about what Seabrook knew and hadn't published yet, worried enough to set up a clumsy scam with a pretty girl as bait.

Then she asked again about what Seabrook knew. They sparred back and forth, and in a few more minutes it was over. Seabrook had no information for her, nor she for him.

She made him walk back to his car, no return ride for him. On the long walk to his truck, he thought there was a kernel of truth in this weird affair. He had long suspected that attorneys did pay hospital workers, especially those in medical records, for information about cases. Perhaps an attorney had hired Lisa and she had worked in Emory's medical-records area. At any rate, she had given him nothing but the conviction that the Cavanagh case was getting sleazier. Somebody was desperate.

* * *

NOVEMBER 1985

Life on the Emory campus had settled down. With David Campbell vanquished and Allen Gammon banished, the remaining faculty focused on patients and research. The department's turmoil had eased, but the legal team was working full time.

The deposition schedule continued. After the depositions by Cavanagh and the Houston family came a parade of outside people, this time Genevieve Switz. After Cavanagh fired her, she had gone to work for an orthopedic surgeon. She was seven months pregnant at the time of her deposition in late November.

This was Taylor Jones' deposition, aimed at building his case against Cavanagh. The trio of Jones, Hunter Allen, and the hospital attorney assembled at 11:00 with Switz and the court reporter. Jones spent the first few hours eliciting testimony from Switz about her observations that African-American and poor patients were placed last on the operative schedule. Further, the eye bank used an objective rating system to rank the quality of the corneal tissue available for transplanting. Switz had noted that the best corneas were used first and the worst-quality tissues used last. A reasonable conclusion: African-American patients and poor white patients got worse tissue and were operated on late in the day, when Dr. Cavanagh and his assistants were fatigued. Switz testified that she had told Allen about this when he interviewed her the previous May.

Hunter Allen must have considered the devastating public-relations problem that the racial element of this case would bring, not to mention the effect on a jury. With a blind, African-American, and obviously poor defendant being led in and out of the courtroom in front of an Atlanta jury, and a white witness testifying that many African-American patients received poor tissue at the end of the day, only the most masochistic of lawyers would relish being on the defense team.

Hunter Allen accused Taylor Jones of advising Mr. Houston not to return to see Cavanagh, with the clear implication that Jones' advice had caused delay in Houston's care and was therefore responsible for Houston's blindness. He also accused Jones of opening his files to Charles Seabrook.

When his time to question came, Allen hammered away at Switz. He asked her if she had let Cavanagh down because she had not looked at the chart after she had injected Houston:

Question by Allen: *So you did not leave the operating room; you went ahead and blocked the eye, and then you turned your attention to the chart in the operating room and finished that up before you left operating room?*

Answer by Switz: *And when I left the operating room, Dr. Newman was in the process of finishing up cutting the corneal button, and Dr. Cavanagh was draping the eye.*

Q: *But he hadn't started the surgery yet, had he?*

A: *No.*

Q: *And if you had looked at the chart then you would have known, wouldn't you, that the wrong eye had been blocked and could have stopped the whole thing, couldn't you?*

A: *I don't know.*

Q: *You don't know?*

A: *I don't know. I think that's an unfair question.*

Q: *Why is it unfair?*

A: *I wasn't doing the surgery.*

Q: *If you had looked at the chart and seen that Mr. Houston was supposed to have his right eye...*

A: *I told you, I didn't look at the operative consent form.*

Q: *The question, ma'am, if you had looked at it, if you had just looked at the op note...*

A: *If I had, I would have been able to tell...*

Q: *Above the page that you were writing on right above where you were writing, you would have known you'd blocked the wrong eye, and you could have stopped the whole thing, isn't that true?*

A: *You're putting words in my mouth.*

Q: *Well, but he depended a lot on you, didn't he?*

A: *Not in circumstances like that.*

Q: *No?*

A: *I don't think so.*

Q: *Didn't he depend on you to see that all the paperwork was in order and consent forms were signed and the history and physical was done and the patient was admitted and the patient was down to the operating room or the holding area; and that the eye was dilated; and that the eyelashes were clipped; and that the eye was blocked; and that the personnel had the operating room scrubbed down, and that the schedule was adhered to as closely...he depended on you for all those things, didn't he?*

A: *And ultimately he is the supervisor.*

Q: *Didn't he depend on you for those things?*

A: *Yes. And ultimately he is the supervisor...*

Q: *And you let him down, didn't you?*
A: *...and responsible.*
Q: *And you let him down in this case, didn't you?*
A: *I think that he was very responsible for how I behaved.*
Q: *But you let him down, didn't you?*
A: *I'm unwilling to say that.*
Q: *Well, do you think you did?*
A: *I don't think so, under the circumstances.*
Q: *You don't? You don't think you let him down when you didn't go back after you blocked the eye and look at the chart?*
A: *I don't know what you're trying to imply.*
Q: *Do you think you let him down when you didn't notice whether the eyelashes were clipped?*
A: *Let's just leave it at I don't think I let him down.*
Q: *Do you think you let him down when you didn't look at the operating schedule as you walked to the door?*
A: *I usually look at the operative permit, not at the operating schedule.*
Q: *Do you think you let him down when you didn't look to see if the eye was dilated before the surgery?*
A: *I told you already, I don't think I let him down.*

On and on it went—hammer, hammer, hammer—Switz resisting, squirming, and uncomfortable in the late stages of her first pregnancy. Six hours had now passed; it was late afternoon, and Allen's questions about the African-American patients had not even begun. He had asked her about other events on the days following Houston's surgery, and she had testified that Newman told her the morning of the 13th, the day after the surgery, that Cavanagh had instructed Newman to tell Houston that they had "decided to operate" on the left eye because it had disease as well.

Switz also said that when she heard that Newman had been instructed to lie, she challenged him to look at the chart with her. She had clearly remembered that the left eye was free of disease. They had then looked at the chart and found several changes, some of which she recognized as Cavanagh's, that had not been there previously. They were clearly late changes in order to justify surgery on an essentially healthy eye.

By 5:30 she had had enough. She forced an adjournment and promised to return on another day. Hunter Allen would be ready for her.

* * *

NOVEMBER 27, 1985

In this month, Emory Clinic finances attracted public attention. The formula for dividing income amongst the doctors was complex and difficult to understand. Dr. Charles Hatcher had been in charge of awarding bonuses for years and had a reputation for giving bigger bonuses to a chosen few than their income production seemed to allow.

Reputedly, one of the chosen was Hatcher himself. He had quit operating on a regular basis in 1983, although he continued to be paid as if he had done surgeries, when in fact one of his cardiac-surgery partners had done the work. In 1983 Hatcher paid himself a salary in excess of a million dollars, a salary that could be regarded as at least five times the reasonable amount for a full-time academic clinic director and would be slightly over $2 million in 2008. So how did he do this? Did he reward his buddies and take from the unfavored doctors on campus? Most of the Emory doctors had no clue and never questioned the process, at least in public. Except one: Dr. William Biggers.

Dr. Biggers was a psychiatrist who had left the Emory faculty for private practice a few years earlier. Hatcher had given Biggers permission to rummage through the financial records of the clinic back when Biggers was a partner in the early '80's. He hadn't paid that much attention or known exactly what Biggers had done.

Biggers had a surprise for Hatcher, though. He understood and had taken exception to Hatcher's financial dealings within the clinic. After looking at tax returns and other records, Biggers fumed and stewed. Four years after he left, shortly before the statute of limitations expired, Biggers took action.

IN THE SUPERIOR COURT OF DEKALB COUNTY
STATE OF GEORGIA

W.L. BIGGERS CIVIL ACTION
NUMBER 85-8735-5
PLAINTIFF VS. C.R. HATCHER
DEFENDANT

SUMMONS TO THE ABOVE NAMED DEFENDANT:

> *You are hereby summoned.....*
> *This 27th day of November, 1985*

After the deputy sheriff left Hatcher's office, you can be sure that Hunter Allen was on the phone within seconds.

The suit had to do with Hatcher's performance as clinic director. It alleged that he had violated the partnership agreement and breached his fiduciary duty to Biggers by:

a. *Failing to make full disclosure of financial information...to Biggers and other partners.*
b. *Allowing certain selected partners to earn income outside of the partnership business, which income should have been partnership income.*
c. *Overcompensating certain administrative employees... and concealing their level of compensation.*

d. *Orchestrating the payment of "administrative" salaries to certain selected partners who actually performed no administrative duties.*

e. *Setting his own administrative salary without the knowledge or consent of the partnership with regard to its amount.*

f. *Overseeing and implementing organizational and structural changes in the partnership in a fashion which effectively concentrated certain selected partners into a highly profitable "sub-partnership" in order to increase Hatcher's own annual income and the income of certain selected partners to the detriment of Biggers and other partners.*

g. *Entering into financial agreements with organizational entities with which the partnership co-existed.*

h. *Soliciting an opinion from the partnership's legal counsel as to Hatcher's duty to Biggers and other partners and ultimately securing an opinion that Hatcher had no duty to release financial records...and further using the partnership's legal counsel, which should have represented Biggers and all partners....to defend Hatcher against any action brought by Biggers.*

When a doctor is sued, the first fear is immediate newspaper publicity. Doctors don't realize how many suits are filed and how non-newsworthy almost every malpractice lawsuit is. Hatcher had experienced enough legal proceedings to know that publicity was not an immediate concern. But he had to be worried about these allegations. This was not a malpractice case; this was a case of misappropriating money. If the allegations were true, he had breached his duty to every Emory Clinic partner, not just to Biggers.

Moreover, even though Biggers' suit covered Hatcher's activities up to 1982, Hatcher had continued to pay himself huge salaries from clinic dollars, consistently in excess of a million dollars. He had been vice president of Health Affairs and had not done surgery on a regular basis since 1983. So how did he get a clinic salary after 1983, after Perdue took over as CEO of the clinic? Dr. Hatcher made himself the chief financial officer for the clinic and kept control of Emory Clinic finances.

What were the facts? Did Biggers have a case? Would word get out? Would the *Atlanta Journal-Constitution* have a field day with another juicy Emory story?

* * *

DECEMBER 2, 1985—MONDAY

Promptly at 11:00 AM, Genevieve Switz entered the conference room in Taylor Jones' office to find not only the three attorneys from her first ordeal, but Dr. Cavanagh as well. Hunter Allen had been busy; he had served her with a subpoena to force her to bring certain records to this deposition. He had known since May that she had kept surgical schedules as well as parts of patient charts, and he wanted to know what she had. He had plans for this information, plans that would involve Switz in ways she had not anticipated. But that would come later. Today he wanted to use certain facts to embarrass and discredit her.

Switz had been trained in statistics. Early on in her job with Cavanagh, when she had formed a general impression about the placement of African-Americans at the end of the day, she had begun keeping the surgery schedule from each of her days and had noted the race of the patients. As she went through each day's schedule, noting the overwhelming number of days when African-Americans were last or near the last, she built an objective case for her impression. Allen had noted that one of the days in her analysis was a day when Stulting, not Cavanagh, was the surgeon. Although the erroneous inclusion of this one day altered the overall statistical analysis not at all, Allen attacked:

Q: *Well, which was it, did Cavanagh do all the cases on October 20, 1983, or did Stulting do them on October 20, 1983?*

A: *I don't remember. We need to check the record.*

Q: *Well, you told Mr. Jones that you were there and you witnessed them personally, each and every case?*

A: *Uh-huh.*

Q: *Is that true?*

A: *Yes.*

Q: *And you told me that earlier today, didn't you?*

A: *Yes. I thought that that was so. I would have to check the clinic record to see whether it was Dr. Stulting's.*

Q: *Can you tell from Exhibit 18 that Stulting did all the cases on October 20, 1983?*

A: *As I say, I'd have to check the clinic record to get the objective data.*

Q: *So you can't tell from Exhibit 18 whether Dr. Cavanagh did any cases on that day, is that true?*

A: *I don't know. I'd have to check the clinic record.*

Q: *Well, are you prepared to swear under oath....*

The questions were nonstop. After Hunter Allen came Mr. Bennett, lawyer for the hospital. He focused on the day of the surgery when she followed Cavanagh's orders to block the eye he pointed to rather than make him wait while she checked the operative permit. Question after question, worded slightly differently, but all the same: Didn't you violate your duty to Dr. Cavanagh by not checking? Didn't you? Didn't you? Didn't you? She could only say no in so many ways. Finally it ended, and she left downtown Atlanta to tend to her life and the birth of her first child.

Genevieve Switz was a crucial witness. She placed the blame for the wrong-eye surgery on the combination of the atmosphere set up by Cavanagh's heavy volume and his direct orders. She had witnessed Dr. Newman lie to Sargus Houston on Cavanagh's orders and had seen the chart changed. Most importantly, she had kept detailed records that demonstrated a racial difference in the order in which surgery was performed and the use of quality corneal tissue. Was there any way to derail her?

* * *

December 1985

Dr. Allen Gammon, true to his earlier promise to David Campbell, continued to work to expose Cavanagh. He told me in a later interview that he employed an "insurgent" strategy: put a bomb in every alley he could find. He didn't know which would explode with the most damage, but surely, he thought, something would. Another alley was the American Academy of Ophthalmology, the highly respected specialty society of U.S. ophthalmologists. Gammon prepared a formal complaint to the ethics committee of the AAO, long and detailed. Although several of his California mentors predicted that the academy would never act, pointing out that department chairs had unlimited and undisputed power, Gammon tried anyway. It couldn't hurt and might help. He mailed the report and made a few phone calls.

* * *

January 1986

The new year should have been as comfortable as the fall of 1985 for Cavanagh and his allies. For the inner circle, yes; for Cavanagh, no. Dr. Z. was causing trouble.

Patients began calling, angry at receiving unsolicited phone calls from attorneys who questioned the care given them by Dr. Cavanagh. One patient, Chris Holcombe (not his real name), was particularly upset. He had called Peggy Brown, Cavanagh's secretary.

He reminded Brown that he lived in a small town, where people were unsophisticated, especially about diseases like herpes, the disease he had. Just the word *herpes* would embarrass Holcombe and hurt his business. He wanted to know how this lawyer had gotten his personal information, who had been looking at his chart, how this could have happened. He wanted to speak to the clinic's lawyer. And Hunter Allen wanted to talk to him; Allen needed help.

Who was the mole? Who the hell was the mole? That's all Charlie Hatcher had wanted to know from David Campbell six months earlier. That's what Cavanagh had wanted to know from Gammon a year earlier—"Were you the one who called 'that black man?'" Now Hunter Allen needed to know.

In Allen's mind, laws were being violated, laws relating to Emory's ownership of patient records and patient confidentiality. He had hammered at Genevieve Switz a month earlier about her retention of surgical schedules and patient charts. Worst of all, it wasn't reporters calling these patients, it was lawyers, lawyers clearly looking for clients so they could add to Emory's misery and file more lawsuits. Allen had his suspicions but no conclusive facts, except for one person—Switz.

He knew Switz had patient records; he knew she had been fired; he knew she was disgusted by the way Cavanagh handled the Houston affair. That was enough. He went to work. He would fix her.

* * *

JANUARY 20, 1986

Taylor Jones was building his case. Today Philip Newman would testify in his deposition. Genevieve Switz had already testified that she had witnessed Newman lying to Houston. What would Dr. Newman say? Would he corroborate? Would he help build the gallows from which Taylor Jones intended to hang Cavanagh?

Newman had his own attorney, Rob Kaufman, whose office was in the Buckhead area, 460 E. Paces Ferry Rd. Jones, Bennett, and Allen's partner, Carlton King, drove out from downtown for a 9:30 date. Newman testified most of the day.

Newman first noted that in a typical ten-case day, he would actually be in the operating room assisting Cavanagh with only a few cases. Switz took Newman's place frequently while Newman attended to other patients or began surgery in another room.

He confirmed that Cavanagh had instructed him to tell Houston that Cavanagh had decided to operate on the left eye and that Newman had done as instructed, both with Houston and with Dorothy Fuller, Houston's niece.

How did Newman decide which patient to put at the end of the day when he would get to perform the surgery? *We generally tried to select people who had a problem we hadn't operated on before and for people who were not—how do I phrase that?—who were not especially well-off, people who were not major contributors to Emory, for example.... Generally on the middle to bottom portion of the* [socioeconomic] *scale.*

Regarding Houston's first operation, Newman had noted that the room was set up for the right eye and that he had been "uncomfortable" that Cavanagh was operating on the left eye. He said nothing to Cavanagh because he assumed Cavanagh knew what he was doing. Furthermore, the room setup was Cavanagh's design, so Cavanagh should have been the first to recognize the error if there was one.

Did Cavanagh change chart entries? Yes, Newman pointed out chart alterations in Houston's chart that, in his opinion, were in Cavanagh's handwriting and were meant to justify, after the fact, surgery on Houston's good eye. Newman also testified that Cavanagh had changed Newman's entries on other patients' records, either changing the pressure or vision measurements.

The case was building. Now a second person had testified that Cavanagh had instructed Newman to lie to the patient, had changed the chart in an effort to deceive, and did allow the disadvantaged patients to be operated on last. These accusations would not look good to a jury. There was only one solution: make sure the jury never saw this testimony.

* * *

FEBRUARY 1986

State boards of medical examiners work in secrecy. Critics hate the lack of transparency, assuming that anything they can't see and monitor isn't being done correctly. But boards do work. In Georgia, the official name is the Composite State Board of Medical Examiners. Governors appoint ten physicians, two osteopaths, one physician's assistant, and one public member. They work with no pay except for minimal expense reimbursement in a thankless job— the job of judging their peers. The Georgia board also administers examinations, issues licenses, and monitors physicians' behavior. Often the board finds minor problems, which are fixed merely by an investigation and a private letter. The ultimate penalty is license revocation, the death penalty for a physician. In the 1980s, state boards rarely communicated with each other, so the loss of a license in one state would occasion a move to another state, a fresh start, and little chance of past sins being discovered. Another option was to allow a physician to move from the state with the understanding that the license would not be renewed in that state.

Dr. Irving Staley, an ophthalmologist and state board member, had told David Campbell eight months earlier that the board expected further action from Emory regarding Cavanagh. Campbell had relayed the warning. Staley had also discussed Cavanagh with Gammon to confirm the rumors about unacceptable practice patterns. Now Staley initiated a Board investigation of Dwight Cavanagh. Campbell met with a committee of the board. Before that meeting, Emory made sure that Campbell was muzzled. In a letter to Campbell's attorney, Hunter Allen spelled out the rules:

February 18, 1986

Dear Penn [Campbell's personal attorney]*:*
It is the position of the Emory Clinic that none of its
partners without prior authorization from the appropriate
managing partners of the clinic should divulge any informa-
tion which was discussed or considered during any peer-
review process, nor should they reveal any of the findings of
the peer-review committees. Specifically, the clinic will trust
Dr. Campbell not to divulge to the State Board of Medical
Examiners or anyone else the information outlined above.

Hunter Allen

Campbell prepared a three-page legal statement for the board
outlining his decision to abide by the clinic's rules even though, *I*
wish to make it clear that I do not wish to be and do not consider
myself as a spokesman for the clinic's position. Moreover, I have
not adopted that position as my own, either as a legal matter or
otherwise. In fact, I have serious questions about that position.

Emory would invoke the protection of peer review to frustrate
not only the state board, but to prevent multiple court hearings from
discovering embarrassing details of the various Cavanagh investigations.

The public could not know the details of Campbell's testimony
or the details of the board's investigation. Allen Gammon talked
frequently with Irving Staley, also. Gammon viewed the board as
another alley for bomb-throwing in his insurgent strategy. One could
guess that the board, charged with protecting the citizens of Georgia
from negligent physicians, disapproved of the actions of Georgia's
premier academic medical center in obstructing the performance of
its duties. Dr. Staley, an eye doctor himself, would advise the board
on the details of eye surgery and the implications of Cavanagh's

behavior. The board was looking into what Cavanagh had done, and it would take action. And Emory knew it.

* * *

FEBRUARY 23, 1986

The Sunday *Atlanta Journal- Constitution* once again delivered a blow to Cavanagh and Emory. Charles Seabrook highlighted the Houston suit in his article about medical mistakes:

Sunday Magazine

MEDICAL MISTAKES: A FACT OF LIFE AND DEATH

Even the best doctors make mistakes. And even the best doctors get sued. Whether doctors are making more mistakes than ever is a matter of conjecture.

By Charles Seabrook/ STAFF

Late in the evening on September 12, 1983, Dr. H. Dwight Cavanagh, a stocky, bespectacled eye surgeon regarded as one of the nation's leading ophthalmologists, walked into operating room number 15 at Emory University Hospital to perform his twelfth operation of the day....

After more discussion of Cavanagh's mistake, accusations of cover-up, and lawsuit, Seabrook turned his focus to medical mistakes in general. Later in the article, he mentioned a child at Emory's Egleston Hospital for Children who had a kidney mistakenly removed instead of a spleen. All in all, it was not the kind of article that would be welcome at any institution, especially Emory. The pressure on Cavanagh and the university went up a notch.

* * *

MARCH 13, 1986

Gladys Wilson hesitated as she entered Taylor Jones' downtown law office. With only one eye, she had to watch carefully when she was in a strange place, or she would trip. Her misery had never ended. After the first Seabrook article, she had tracked Jones down and sent him a copy of her Emory records. Now, months later, after prodding from her family, she met Jones for the first time. After getting a glass of water, she faced Jones and told him she was angry and upset. She was blind in one eye and hadn't driven since before the first surgery. They had put her through hell with all those operations and pain.

She told Taylor Jones that the anesthesia from the first retina operation had made her sick, and they wouldn't listen when it came time for the second one. Dr. Kaplan just said it wasn't his department. He didn't seem to care. So she got just as sick after the second one. She knew that didn't help the operation for her to just lie there throwing up right after the surgery was done.

She detailed the misery of Cavanagh's patient days, how she and her mother would sit on those hard wooden chairs from 1:00 to 5:00 or 6:00, afraid to go to the bathroom or get something to eat. If they called you, you better be ready to go. She told how Cavanagh would see her mother for a few minutes and then Wilson, saying only that God had cursed their family, that her eyes were just like her mother's.

She related how she had told Cavanagh that she didn't want Dr. Leaper in the operating room and produced a bill for $490 ($1077 in 2008) for his assisting. When she asked Dr. Cavanagh, he denied it at first and then said he hadn't let Dr. Leaper do anything, which made Wilson wonder why he sent a bill. On Wilson's Emory chart, Cavanagh's operative note didn't list an assistant. Wilson wondered how a doctor could get away with billing for an assisting physician when that doctor hadn't done any of the work.

Jones finally got through with some questions of his own, and then it was settled: Wilson would sue Cavanagh. Wilson signed the contract, and Jones began to draft. He'd heard it all before.

It didn't take Jones long, but he added a wrinkle in this suit, a new allegation. He sued Emory University as the owner of the Emory University Hospital; he sued the clinic; and he sued Cavanagh, alleging violation of the racketeering statutes. The common term was "RICO," the acronym for the Federal Racketeering Influenced & Corrupt Organizations Act. Moreover, he filed the suit in federal court, avoiding what he would later allege as undue favoritism toward Emory by the superior-court judge hearing the Houston suit.

The theory of the racketeering charge was that both the hospital and the clinic knew of Cavanagh's unnecessary surgery and fraudulent billing of assistant's fees but had failed to intervene because both entities profited from the fees generated. The penalty for racketeering: triple payment of damages awarded. Jones had raised the stakes. Did he have a case?

* * *

Sunday, March 30, 1986

The Atlanta Journal-Constitution

EMORY'S CHIEF EYE SURGEON FACES THIRD SUIT

By Charles Seabrook, Science/Medicine/STAFF

A third medical malpractice lawsuit has been filed against Dr. H. Dwight Cavanagh, the chairman of Emory University's ophthalmology department, alleging that he performed unnecessary surgery on a Decatur woman and billed her for medical services that were never performed....

MARCH 31, 1986—MONDAY

On March 31, a representative of the American Academy of Ophthalmology called Charles Hatcher, informing him that the ethics committee of the AAO would perform a formal ethics-committee hearing of Dwight Cavanagh.

Dr. Hatcher could protect Cavanagh no longer. He called Cavanagh, who was on vacation, to demand that he take a leave of absence. He could not even return to his office to collect his personal items. Cavanagh now had three lawsuits—the state board and today the American Academy of Ophthalmology. He would need to concentrate on his defense.

Cavanagh would be on indefinite leave, without prejudice, with full pay, but he could not show his face on the Emory campus. If he were cleared in the various investigations, he could come back.

Emory began a series of efforts, shrouded in secrecy, to head off the academy's ethics investigation. One letter, from Dr. James McCulley, chairman of ophthalmology at the University of Texas, Southwestern, to president Jim Laney, alludes to Emory's activities: *I would like to compliment you on what has been resistance to an apparent inappropriate intrusion by the American Academy of Ophthalmology into academic, university, affairs. I am very embarrassed to be a member of the academy at this time and am not at all supportive, much less proud of the organization's behavior. I am delighted that you at Emory did not yield to pressure and that you maintained a strong and appropriate stand....*

Could Emory head off the academy's investigation and get Cavanagh off his leave?

* * *

April 1, 1986—Tuesday

The Atlanta Journal-Constitution

HEAD OF EMORY OPTHALMOLOGY [SIC] *TAKING LEAVE UNTIL SUITS SETTLED*

By Charles Seabrook Science/Medicine/STAFF

Dr. H. Dwight Cavanagh, head of Emory University's ophthalmology department and a defendant in three pending malpractice suits, will accept an indefinite leave of absence pending resolution of his legal problems, Emory officials said Monday.

"We have been verbally advised by Dr. Cavanagh that he will accept an immediate leave of absence," said Dr. Garland Perdue, head of Emory University Clinic, where Cavanagh practices.

Cavanagh could not be reached for comment.

Perdue said Cavanagh was out of the state Monday and "dictated" his plans by phone to Emory officials, who had suggested that the eye doctor take a leave of absence until his legal difficulties are resolved....

Cavanagh, chairman of the department since 1978, also is under investigation by the Composite State Board of Medical Examiners for alleged wrongful medical practice. If the board determines that Cavanagh violated state medical practice laws, it could suspend or revoke his license....

Curiously, the results of Cavanagh's "dictation" never reached the desks of Perdue or Hatcher, at least not for many months.

Doctors Campbell and Gammon were relieved but certainly not celebrating. Gammon hoped that Cavanagh's departure would increase his options to remain at Emory with his research team, enabling him to continue his academic career. Campbell was more sober. He knew the resources at Cavanagh's command, even when he was out of the office. Campbell was finishing out his year at Emory, still seeing patients, but he did not yet have a job, and the prospects were poor. He reminded Gammon that the interim chairman, Dr. Louis Wilson, was not Gammon's friend.

* * *

APRIL 16, 1986

Allen Gammon rushed in, late by ten minutes, to the Emory Clinic partners' meeting, called by Dr. Garland Perdue to discuss the suits against Dwight Cavanagh and the clinic. As usual, Dr. Gammon taped this meeting and the one with Charles Hatcher later that day. On the stage with Dr. Perdue were Mr. Roy Townsend, the clinic executive, and one of attorney Hunter Allen's partners. Travis Meredith, Henry Kaplan, and Louis Wilson sat together in the front row. At least fifty physician partners listened as Dr. Perdue discussed the outstanding suits and the racketeering charges against them all.

A psychiatrist asked if he were liable since he had never seen the patients who were suing and was told yes, he was a partner and was liable and could have his personal possessions attacked. The clinic had $30–$40 million in insurance coverage, but it was uncertain whether fraudulent billing was covered.

Garland Perdue labeled the suits as trumped-up and inexcusable. The allegations had been looked into by the Department of Ophthalmology and then the Professional Standards and Ethics Committee, composed of senior members of the clinic, and he would defend their findings to his last breath.

Another partner offered a formal motion that the clinic authorize its counsel to investigate members of the clinic under oath so they could determine who was aiding the attorneys in filing these suits.

The doctor sitting next to Gammon leaned over to Gammon to warn him they were talking about him. Gammon would need some defense.

Allen Gammon knew that Emory was targeting him. For the past few months, he believed that private detectives tailed him when he was driving. He was convinced that his secretary was a spy for Hunter Allen and part of her job was to rummage through his effects and monitor his phone calls. He had begun walking across the street to a pay phone inside a hotel to make sensitive calls.

Immediately following the unusual partnership meeting, Gammon walked with Charles Hatcher to Hatcher's office and taped their conversation:

Gammon: *Let me come to my bottom line.... I want full reinstatement of all the things that have been done to me....*

Hatcher: *I don't think anybody has taken anything away from you.*

Gammon: *I certainly would say so. I think when all your titles are removed, when your practice, your equipment, your personal effects are dumped into a box and you're evicted from your place of work in a partnership in which you are a member, when allegations are made about you, aspersions cast to your...patients.*

On and on, back and forth, Hatcher contended that all committees had found Cavanagh blameless and that Gammon and Campbell stood alone in opposition. Neither one convinced the other, and Hatcher finally said, *I've heard enough about this Dwight Cavanagh to last me a lifetime.*

And so ended Gammon's attempt to convince the top man on campus to reinstate him. Moreover, the partnership meeting made it clear. Dr. Gammon was a target, and the Emory Clinic was the shooter.

* * *

LATE APRIL 1986

Dwight Cavanagh busied himself with his defense in the months during his leave of absence. In a 1987 deposition, Taylor Jones asked what he had been doing:

Q (by Mr. Jones): *Under what circumstances did you take a leave of absence from Emory Clinic and Emory University on or about April 1, 1986?*

A (by Cavanagh): *Let's go slowly on this one. I took a leave of absence on April the 1ˢᵗ, 1986, from Emory University and Emory Clinic to prepare my defense carefully, meticulously, against one of the most unprovoked, vicious, malicious types of personal attacks that I have ever heard of or encountered in medicine in this century by Mr. Taylor Jones.*

Q: *You're referring to me in my capacity as attorney for the plaintiff in lawsuit, I presume?*

A: *No, I am referring to and I wish to state at the outset this is my belief. I'm not accusing Mr. Jones of anything. These are my beliefs.*

At the present time, I'm using this opportunity of time since April 1 to acquire evidence in support of these beliefs and in no way wish to impugn the honesty and integrity of Mr. Jones, but wish to state this period of time is being utilized to pursue the following train of thought: That Mr. Jones, acting in conjunction with party or parties, known and unknown, both professional employees, former and current, of Emory University and nonprofessional employees, has engaged in a systematic attempt to destroy me personally and professionally. I believe this to be true....

Mr. Allen: *Let's take a break. Dwight, let me talk to you.*

After the break, Jones asked Cavanagh about the late March, 1986, conversation with Charles Hatcher regarding the leave of absence.

Cavanagh: *And I said, well, it's obvious to me that once publication of unsubstantiated allegations surface on the front page of a newspaper, that for a person in public office, public life, as I am, it has to be answered carefully, and that that is going to take up a tremendous amount of time and emotional energy, which is definitely going to interfere with my relationship with my department, which comprises almost 300 employees, five major teaching hospitals, and all the responsibilities I had.*

And I said, I would like some time to think about it and prepare an adequate defense. I don't think it's fair to my department, to my students, to my residents, to my fellows, to my colleagues, not to do that.

This is so devastating personally and emotionally, devastating psychologically, mentally, every way, to have this type of thing come out in the paper, that it needs to be carefully answered.

He [Hatcher] said, I will certainly support you in requesting that necessary leave of absence, which I did in writing within the next two days when I got back.

* * *

MAY 15, 1986

The legal work only got worse. Hunter Allen busied himself primarily with the defense of the three lawsuits, but he was also planning an offensive move as well, determined to expose the person who leaked the information to Taylor Jones.

The patients had continued to call, all angry at getting phone calls from attorneys who knew about the problems with their eye care. No one knew the informant, and Allen wanted to lob a grenade into an alley and see what came their way.

But today came Gladys Wilson for the deposition in her suit against Cavanagh.

The gathering at Taylor Jones' office for Wilson's deposition included Dwight Cavanagh.

Gladys Wilson, calm and articulate, painted a devastating picture of her care, or lack thereof, as well as her mother's.

In respect to her mother:

Q: *Do you remember anything that was objectionable in your mind about the way he [Cavanagh] talked to your mom or the way he examined her?*

A: *No, except for the shortness of the examination.*

Q: *All right. Did you feel like Dr. Cavanagh's exams were not thorough enough?*

A: *I felt that he did not spend enough time with his patients.*

Q: *Did you complain to him about that?*

A: *No.*

Q: *Did you complain to anybody at Emory about that feeling?*

A: *Just the people sitting around in the waiting rooms. We all complained.*

Q: *All right. Did you ever have the feeling during these visits to Dr. Cavanagh that Dr. Cavanagh was trying to force treatment on your mom or trying to propose treatment that she didn't need?*

A: *Well, I'll have to answer that this way. I don't know whether you would call it force or not, but he painted a rosy picture, which would naturally, if you believed it, you would—would you call that force?*

Q: *No, but it doesn't matter what I call anything. What I meant by—*

A: *But if somebody paints you a rosy picture and says let's do this and this will all be beautiful, well then, naturally, I would go along with it.*

Q: *All right. Did you ever feel like Dr. Cavanagh was seeing your mother too frequently to run up his charges?*

A: *Yes.*

Q: *When did you come to that feeling?*
A: *We felt that every time we went over there.*

The focus turned to her own care, and after several more hours came the question:

Q: *Do you believe that Dr. Cavanagh deliberately tried to hurt you in any way at any time in his medical care?*
A: *I believe that he unnecessarily operated on me and didn't take the proper care of me during the operation or after the operation.*
Q: *All right. And my question—*
A: *When, evidently, something went wrong.*
Q: *Yes, ma'am. I'm asking you what you believe. Do you believe that he did those things deliberately?*
A: *I think the corneal transplant was a deliberate operation.*
Q: *Okay.*
A: *That was not required.*
Q: *And I assume, then, it's your belief that he was deliberately trying to harm you by doing that procedure? Is that what you believe?*
A: *The word "harm," I don't know how you use it that way.... The only thing I can answer you is that...he deliberately did an unnecessary operation on my eye and that he did not follow up after something happened during the operation, and I was not told what happened, and I was not given any information afterwards.*

Add to this the testimony that she had not driven and her husband had to quit his job to help take care of her mother. Chalk her up as another one Hunter Allen likely hoped would never see the light of day before a jury.

* * *

MAY 23, 1986

Hunter Allen at last got to go on the offensive. He had convinced himself that the leak of patient information came from Genevieve Switz, so he filed suit against her.

A panicked Switz called Taylor Jones to inform him of the suit and the allegations that she had illegally obtained Emory records and given them to others. Emory wanted the records returned and a fine paid.

Switz faced more legal bills and the potential for a judgment against her, all more than she could afford. Jones knew that he couldn't represent her, but he volunteered to find her an attorney and get him to work with her on the bill.

Since he first started on the Sargus Houston case in 1985, Jones had received so many requests to sue Cavanagh that he couldn't handle all the patients. He farmed out some of the work to other attorneys but kept himself on each case as co-counsel. That way all the attorneys could share information and coordinate strategy, especially the RICO charges. An attorney named Charles McCranie was working on another case. He knew all the details. He would be a good one for Switz.

Hunter Allen's case against Switz seemed to sink into a muddy pit after just two depositions. In their depositions, both Switz and Jones denied ever sharing information. Switz didn't have addresses of patients, only surgical schedules and snippets of other charts she had kept as part of her job. About half of Emory Hospital had access to surgery schedules, so she certainly didn't have unique information. She did have Sargus Houston's chart, but so did many other people.

Despite successful depositions, Switz faced a jury trial. Did Hunter Allen hope that the specter of her own future trial would influence her testimony in the Houston case?

* * *

JUNE 1986

Dr. Louis Wilson, now interim chairman of ophthalmology, wreaked the ultimate revenge on Allen Gammon by simply firing him. The letter arrived at Gammon's bare-bones office at Crawford Long Hospital in June. Wilson didn't even give Gammon the courtesy of a face-to-face meeting. Gammon was gone. He shouldn't have been surprised, but he was. His career at Emory was finished. His home, no more. Gammon began scrambling.

* * *

JULY 1986

From Dwight Cavanagh's perspective, July brought some good news. Both David Campbell and Allen Gammon had left Atlanta.

Dr. Gammon's departure was more important than Campbell's. Gammon had needed a place to practice, and soon. Dr. Wilson's firing of Gammon was papered as a leave of absence, but all parties knew that Gammon would not be returning to Emory, at least in a full-time capacity. So Gammon had secured a position as chief of pediatric ophthalmology and strabismus at the King Kahled Eye Specialist Hospital in Riyadh, Saudi Arabia. The typical contract for a doctor in Saudi Arabia prohibited home-leave for three months. Despite Emory's posturing, the American Academy of Ophthalmology planned a full-scale ethics-committee investigation in early September. Now that the official accuser, Allen Gammon, was prohibited by his contract from traveling, and thus could not attend the hearing, perhaps the matter could be dropped. Cavanagh and Emory began lobbying again.

Cavanagh campaigned on several fronts. In addition to conducting his legal defense and attempting to cancel the ethics-committee hearing, he used his contacts across the country to pressure the Emory hierarchy. The chairman of Harvard's eye department, Claes

Dohlman, sent the following letter to seventy-one ophthalmologists around the country, many of them department chairs or other leaders, urging that letters of support for Cavanagh be sent to Dr. Richard Krause, Emory's new medical-school dean, with copies to Laney and Hatcher:

*HARVARD MEDICAL SCHOOL * MASSACHUSETTS EYE AND EAR INFIRMARY*

DEPARTMENT OF OPHTHALMOLOGY
Claes Dohlman, M.D.
Professor and Chairman

Dear XXX:

I am sure that you are aware of the extraordinary events that have plagued Emory's fine eye department for the last year or two. There have been allegations against Dwight Cavanagh.... He has come under attack from two faculty members, now departed, who have used exceptional methods in trying to discredit him. The net result is that Dwight is staying at home on "indefinite sabbatical leave," waiting for the outcome of an Academy Ethics Committee report (instigated by his two accusers)....

I personally feel that Dwight—guilty or not of alleged deficiencies—has not deserved the treatment he has received. After all, he has built up Emory's eye department with extraordinary leadership.... I feel strongly that he should be reinstated as chairman as soon as possible.... I have written a letter of strong support for Dwight.... I am now asking you (plus several other academic leaders...)...to write a letter to that effect. I feel that Dwight is a very fine person, a good friend, and an exceptional academic leader who now needs some support from his friends.

Sincerely,
Claes

* * *

The American Academy's ethics-committee chairman tapped a Philadelphia ophthalmologist, George Spaeth, to head the investigation of Dwight Cavanagh. Dr. Spaeth, then 55, had ophthalmology in his blood. Both his father and older brother were ophthalmologists. Born in Philadelphia, he had trained and stayed at the venerable Wills Hospital, one of the world's leading eye centers. Spaeth—slender, erect, and conservative to the bone—exuded ethics. Painstakingly correct in written and spoken word, he, like David Campbell, modeled the ideal for physician behavior. Spaeth was like the majority of physicians in this country. Not flashy, not egotistical, he didn't have to be the first to comment at grand rounds; he didn't have to jump from his seat to offer the first cutting remark. Thoughtful and temperate, he did share the prevailing view of cheaters—he hated them.

Unaware of Gammon's travel prohibition, Spaeth had already set the hearing for early September in Atlanta. With Gammon—the official accuser in the ethics complaint—in Saudi Arabia, would Cavanagh's supporters derail the academy's train?

* * *

AUGUST 1986

Allen Gammon was scrambling again, this time trying to leave Saudi Arabia, not get there. When he heard about the September ethics-committee hearing, he realized that his absence might jeopardize the academy's efforts. After all, if the accuser can't make it to the hearing, what kind of hearing is it for the subject of the complaint, Dwight Cavanagh? True enough, the Saudis' strict rule allowed no departures for three months, but perhaps Gammon could beat that rule. After all, the American Academy of Ophthalmology was really the World Academy of Ophthalmology. Ophthalmologists all over the globe revered the American academy as much as their United States colleagues. For many foreign eye specialists, a visit to the annual meeting of the academy highlighted their career. Moreover, a U.S. ophthalmologist would make the decision. Perhaps Gammon could broker that respect into a suspension of the rule. Perhaps he would get to testify.

* * *

SEPTEMBER 1986

The academy troops arrived in hot, humid Atlanta to pursue the most delicate ethics-committee hearing in academy history. Ethics "challenges," the academy's term for a member's complaint and committee hearings, usually involved controversy over misleading physician advertising or gross negligence on the part of a doctor and rarely centered on a doctor in a university setting. The academy published sanitized results from its ethics-committee deliberations in its newspaper, the *Argus*. Most of the reports involved a doctor giving up his academy membership after losing his license to practice or some such. More commonly, an offending doctor would have to stop advertising deceptively in his local area.

You could ask, what's the big deal? The worst penalty the ethics committee could impose is revocation of academy membership. A doctor does not have to be a member of the academy to get a license or to practice, so there is no immediate financial implication of loss of such membership. Nonmembers can even attend the annual meeting just by paying a higher fee.

But for Dwight Cavanagh, M.D., PhD, trained at the top institutions of the world, desiring to return to his chairmanship at Emory, an adverse ruling, especially if coupled with expulsion from the academy, would kill his career. He would lose face, academic stature, academic advancement, and standing in the hierarchy of organized medicine. This hearing was life or death for Cavanagh.

Spaeth and his team were not judging an eye doctor from a small town who sent out solicitation letters to the townsfolk. They were judging someone with whom the leaders of ophthalmology collaborated at the highest levels, the head of several national committees and chairman of an up-and-coming academic center. They were judging one of their own, a "higher-up." But if anyone thought or hoped that George Spaeth would give Cavanagh a pass because of his stature, he hoped in vain.

The committee hearing would begin on Thursday, September 11. The bombshell struck on Wednesday. On this day the Emory troops heard that Allen Gammon was flying in from Saudi Arabia. Gammon had appealed the rule in the contract prohibiting a leave in the first ninety days, prevailed, dug into his own pocket for airfare, and flown to Atlanta.

Even though he had not sold his home, Gammon reported to the hotel room assigned him by the academy. There he awaited the summons to the committee. He was ready. He had reviewed his written complaint and all the documents he had saved. He didn't really need to reread this; the facts were burned into his soul.

He waited, and no summons came. He waited some more. Finally the phone rang, and George Spaeth dropped his own bomb. The hearing was over. The committee didn't need to talk to Gammon. The matter had been resolved. Spaeth thanked Gammon for returning to Atlanta and seemed apologetic that Gammon had come so far and was not asked to testify. Gammon would hear from the academy later.

Gammon—exhausted, jet-lagged, and somewhat addled—couldn't believe it. He couldn't really take it in. He had pulled strings, paid out considerable dollars, made a big sacrifice, and nobody wanted to talk to him. What about David Campbell? He had flown in from New Hampshire and was waiting. Same deal. No need to talk to him either.

* * *

Indeed, what did happen? Ethics-committee deliberations are confidential, and no one but the participants knows the exact sequence of events. In my interview with him, George Spaeth, respecting the doctrine of confidentiality, could provide only the most general of comments about the investigation: The complaint sent to the academy seemed legitimate, so Spaeth was assigned as the investigator. When Spaeth came to Atlanta, he spoke with Cavanagh and most of the department's faculty, at least those involved in the previous hearings. He remembers Emory as being very cooperative during these times. Nick Chivalis, Cavanagh's personal attorney, was very helpful, especially in convincing Cavanagh that the academy was not being punitive but acting in the best interest of its members.

What happened was the academy's version of a plea bargain, termed an "alternative disposition." Without holding an official ethics-committee hearing, the committee met with Cavanagh and indicated that ethics violations had occurred, and Cavanagh agreed to a series of measures aimed at protecting patients and reversing the damage he had meted to his colleagues. He had to withdraw from practice for two years and from academy activities for one year. He would have to write letters to colleagues he had damaged and agree to have his practice monitored for three years when he resumed seeing patients.

Months later, the following was published in *Argus*:

Argus, May 1987-page 10

ALTERNATIVE DISPOSITION ISSUED UNDER CODE OF ETHICS

When the academy's ethics committee is presented with a challenge to a member, the administrative procedures of the Code of Ethics provide for a carefully constructed review process. At the end of this process (or indeed during it) there may be a number of determinative dispositions....

The following is an actual but anonymous alternative disposition that is presented for its educational value....

The ethics committee was confronted with a complaint alleging violations of Rules 4,5,6, and 9 of the Code of Ethics. The conduct which formed the basis of the complaint included: (a) failure to refer patients for consultation in a timely manner; (b) mistakes in clinical judgment resulting from a physical or mental impairment; (c) unnecessary surgery; (d) alteration of patient charts; and (e) irregularities in billing.

The committee investigated the situation. The investigation indicated violations of the Code of Ethics. However, the investigation also indicated that an alternative disposition that allowed the ethics committee to monitor the practice of the member was in the best interest of patient care. Therefore no formal hearing was held, and the ophthalmologist and the academy agreed to the following...:

1. *The ophthalmologist assured the academy that the conduct involved is not presently occurring and will not occur in the future;*
2. *The ophthalmologist withdrew from clinical and surgical practice for a specified period of time;*
3. *The ophthalmologist, if he decides to re-enter clinical and surgical practice, will submit to a mechanism.... The mechanism will provide for prospective, concurrent, and retrospective monitoring of any patient care...for at least three years.*

No names were given in the article, but to those familiar with the Emory situation, only one person in the United States could have been the subject of this alternative disposition: Dwight Cavanagh, M.D., PhD. Cavanagh had avoided the death penalty, but he had been punished and his behavior deemed unacceptable and a violation of academy ethics. For the first time, an inquiry had supported Allen Gammon and David Campbell.

* * *

OCTOBER 9, 1986

Not even Dwight Cavanagh could withstand such a ruling by the academy—whatever it was called—multiple malpractice lawsuits, and an investigation by the state licensing board. His pals could protect him no longer. When an outside body of your peers with the academy's stature rules against you, you have no recourse. On this date, Cavanagh's letter of resignation—the letter he hoped never to write—appeared on the desk of Dean Krause. The resignation was effective for September 1987, one year hence, and he would remain on a leave of absence with pay until then.

Dr. Krause immediately accepted, and Dwight Cavanagh's career at Emory ended. Cavanagh accepted a research position at Georgetown University and moved out of Atlanta.

With this, a tragic chapter in Emory's history closed.

Emory's administration carried on, happy to have this mess out of its hair and off the front page, or so it hoped. The damaged careers, at least for some, never recovered. The lawyers feasted on, reaping fees for eleven more years. And the damaged patients still woke up blind.

EPILOGUE: THE AFTERMATH

After Cavanagh's resignation, peace settled on the Emory campus. The search committee selected a new chairman from the University of Wisconsin, Dr. Thomas Aaberg, Sr., a match for Cavanagh's intelligence and academic standing. Calm, deliberate, and unruffled, Aaberg healed the department and town relations. He continued building the department, both in substance and in reputation. Emory's eye program now ranks in the top fifteen in the country, and hundreds of medical students vie for the five residency slots every year. One cannot imagine that Aaberg would brook the slightest impropriety on his watch.

While the campus recovered, the legal feast accelerated.

Four patients in addition to Sargus Houston, Gladys Wilson, and Mattie Sue Brown sued Cavanagh and Emory. All seven alleged RICO violations in addition to malpractice, fraud, and other counts. With the exception of Houston's suit, Dr. Cavanagh and Emory settled the suits without trial for undisclosed amounts in 1988.

Sargus Houston's lawsuit meandered through the legal system, stymied by Hunter Allen's desperate attempts to keep documents related to peer-review out of the public eye. Taylor Jones, lead attorney for Houston, contended that the Emory-generated publicity of the Tindall Committee's findings abrogated Emory's rights to keep the supporting details from the public. The courts eventually disagreed with Jones' view and kept faculty members from testifying to any details brought up in any committee meeting, even if they learned the details outside a peer-review process.

Showtime in the Houston case came in 1990, seven years after Houston's first surgery. After opening statements in the first trial, the judge declared a mistrial and fined Jones for contempt after Jones alleged a racial bias in Cavanagh's surgical scheduling. At the second trial, David Campbell was beginning his testimony when the proceedings were abruptly adjourned for the day. On the following day, the parties announced a settlement. Emory would pay Houston a total of $4.2 million (a sum worth $7 million in 2008 dollars). The Sargus Houston saga had ended.

While the main course of the legal feast ended with the Houston settlement, a multicourse dessert extended the lawyers' repast another seven years with lawsuits by David Campbell and Allen Gammon. The lawyers were fat indeed by 1997, when Dr. Cavanagh and Emory settled with both plaintiffs for undisclosed amounts.

David Campbell joined the faculty of Dartmouth Medical School after spending some time, like Gammon, in Saudi Arabia. Garland Perdue wrote him in November 1986:

There is a consensus of opinion that you did act as a matter of conscience. There is no question being raised as to your honesty or motivation. Your skills as an academician and clinician are unquestioned. Your colleagues in ophthalmology hold no ill feelings and wish you well. Other colleagues in other departments similarly are completely willing to let bygones be bygones and do wish you well.

It is perhaps regrettable that other participants in prolongation of the controversy were not identified as a consequence of their being secretive and certainly less open in the matter than you. Some of these are individuals not associated with the university, and others are no longer associated with the university. Therefore, no purpose will be served by any pursuit of the matter. It is clear, however, that you bear less responsibility for prolongation of the controversy than others, perhaps including some of the principals.

You are aware of my personal good will and of my willingness to recommend, endorse, or support your candidacy for academic positions you may seek.

Curiously, despite the warm feelings expressed in this letter and verbally to David Campbell, Perdue refused to lift the reprimand.

Along with his practice, David Campbell pursued his lawsuit against Emory, Cavanagh, et al until its conclusion in 1997 with the payment of an undisclosed amount to both Campbell and Gammon. The losers, in addition to Campbell and his family, are the huge number of people with glaucoma who could have benefited from Campbell's research. Only recently, in 2004, have his research "juices" begun to flow again and have lead him to resume his career of outstanding research.

Allen Gammon entered private practice in Modesto, California, after a year in Saudi Arabia. He continued his research at Emory, flying in from California on a regular basis. When he filed his lawsuit, however, his research at Emory ended.

The chairman of the eye department at Georgetown University, a cornea colleague, kindly hired Dwight Cavanagh to join the faculty. He honored the academy agreement and did not see patients for two years. Several years later, he accepted a position at the University of Texas, Southwestern, in Dallas, taking with him a significant portion of Georgetown's cornea-research team and attendant grants. Cavanagh left behind a gutted cornea section.

Cavanagh rose through the ranks in Dallas and served as associate dean of clinical services for the medical school and medical director of the Zale Lipshy University Hospital. Currently (2009), he holds the Dr. W. Thomas Maxwell chair in ophthalmology and is vice chairman of the department.

Has Cavanagh changed? Compare his answer to the same question posed to him in two lawsuits, one the Houston suit and the other eight years later. First, Dr. Cavanagh's answer to Taylor Jones in a 1987 deposition:

Q (by Mr. Jones): *Under what circumstances did you take a leave of absence from Emory Clinic and Emory University on or about April 1, 1986?*

A (by Cavanagh): *Let's go slowly on this one: I took a leave of absence on April the 1st, 1986, from Emory University and Emory Clinic to prepare my defense carefully, meticulously, against one of the most unprovoked, vicious, malicious type of personal attacks that I have ever heard of or encountered in medicine in this century by Mr. Taylor Jones.*

In 1995 Cavanagh was the defendant in yet another lawsuit, this one filed in Washington, D.C., alleging malpractice in Cavanagh's care of a Georgetown patient. During his deposition, under oath, Cavanagh described his activities at Emory:

Cavanagh: *In 1978 I was promoted to professor and chairman of the department....*

Q (by the attorney): *And you remained that until '86?*

A (by Cavanagh): *Correct. '87, I believe. I don't remember the exact date I decided to step down.... In 1986 I decided to take a sabbatical year. This normally occurs about every seven years for many academics, and I decided to relinquish my responsibilities as professor and chairman and accept employment at Georgetown.*

Oh? Charles Hatcher had a different view.

In a deposition in 1989, Dr. Hatcher discussed the circumstances of Cavanagh's leave of absence:

Q (by attorney to Hatcher): *Do you recall the leave of absence he took on that date?*

A (by Hatcher): *Yes, I recall his leave of absence.*

Q: *Was that voluntary on the part of Dr. Cavanagh?*

A: *Well, I suggested he take a leave of absence, and he agreed it was the appropriate thing to do. That was on the date that I received a call on behalf of the American Academy of Ophthalmology that it was their intent for their ethics committee to conduct an audit of Dr. Cavanagh's practice.*

I appreciated the notification, and I immediately notified him that, pending the investigation, I felt that he should not be involved in activities here and that I'd like for him to take a leave of absence without prejudice with full pay until the matter was resolved.... If any organization of the stature of the College of Ophthalmology [sic] feels inclined to conduct an inquiry, until the conclusions are made available to me, I did not wish that particular individual to take any kind of actions.

Q: *Was it your intention at the time that the leave of absence would be a permanent departure for Dr. Cavanagh, or was that question reserved?*

A: *That question was reserved.*

Hatcher phrased it this way in a 1992 deposition, referring to the leave of absence: *You didn't read me. I said I advised him in a way in which he clearly understood that's what he was to do.*

If the leave of absence wasn't voluntary, what about the decision to resign? Now, back to Cavanagh's 1995 Washington deposition:

Q: *Did you leave Emory as a result of any medical malpractice claim against you?*

A: *I didn't leave Emory because of any medical malpractice claim against me, no.*

Q: *Were you caused to leave?*

A: *No.*

Q: *Your leaving was totally voluntary?*

A: *It certainly was.*

In Charles Hatcher's 1989 deposition, he hedged on exactly how "voluntary" Cavanagh's resignation was:

Q: *Did Dr. Cavanagh finally make his resignation permanent in October 1986, to the best of your recollection?*
A: *Well, I don't recall the exact date. As I recall, it was the recommendation of the college and Dr. Cavanagh, for whatever reasons without any judgment on their part, the circumstances of all that had happened to him had produced significant emotional trauma and agitation on his part, and they felt he probably would be well advised not to conduct the care of patients during a period of time to give himself an opportunity to recover.*
Q: *Who felt that?*
A: *The College of Ophthalmology. It was my understanding that they recommended a period of time in which he not be involved in patient care.*
Q: *Is that the same as the American Academy of Ophthalmology?*
A: *American Academy, yes, I'm sorry. I'm not an ophthalmologist, and I don't always get their organizations right.*
Q: *Is it correct, then, that Dr. Cavanagh's resignation was not voluntary, but was a result of the finding of the American Academy?*
A: *I have no idea why he, you know, what entered his mind, but it was voluntary as far as his letter to me or to us.*
Q: *Would Dr. Cavanagh have been allowed to remain here as chairman of the department in lieu of resigning?*
A: *I can't really tell you what I might have decided faced with that circumstance. I didn't have to face that; he sent me a letter of resignation.*

In a 1991 deposition, Cavanagh testified that his personal effects remained in the chairman's office at Emory until September of 1987:

Q: *Why didn't you go to the eye center and pack up your belongings in your office?*

A: *Because there always remained the possibility, Mr. Butler [attorney for Campbell and Gammon], that I may come back.... I obviously would have packed my things up the instant that things were totally irretrievable, but I believe it was done in fairness to me until the end of August '87 to give the situation a change [sic] to even possibly retrieve itself.*

Q: *So up until August and September of '87, you still thought you might come back to Emory?*

A: *I thought that there was a much—very much of a long shot but, you know, possibility, remote perhaps. But one always retains some hope.*

Q: *Well, why was that hope a long shot?*

A: *Because the controversy just continued, Mr. Butler. People continued the controversy legally, and it widened into different forms. And there was still throughout the United States a constant comment of licenses lost, can't practice, terrible things. There was just continuing, continuing, continuing, widening, deepening.*

Q: *In what way in 1987 up until August and September of '87 did the controversy continue and widen and deepen?*

A: *Well, when I met with Taylor on, I believe, the 2nd of February, 1987, he informed me the FBI was involved. And then in Dr. Gammon's deposition in Modesto recently we find confirmed that he was involved not only with them....*

So was Cavanagh's resignation voluntary? After a frenzied and failed letter-writing campaign, an adverse ruling by the academy, and a deal struck with the state board, he resigned. It was voluntary in the same sense that a condemned man might climb the stairs to the gallows rather than being carried, but even Cavanagh knew when he was defeated.

George Waring shed light on some of Dwight Cavanagh's activities in the early years after he left Emory:

February 24, 1987

Dear Dwight,

When you recruited me to come to the eye department at Emory in 1979, I told you that one major difficulty might characterize our work and relationship: you do not listen to people. Periodically since then, to try to get through to you, I have written letters explaining my thoughts in detail; you have seldom responded.

I must now write again.... A number of our mutual friends in ophthalmology have told me you said that I was largely or partially responsible for your being asked to leave Emory. I strongly object to your saying this to people for two reasons.

The first reason is that it is not true.... The second reason is that the statement is misleading.... You alone, Dwight, are responsible for the difficulties that you encountered at Emory. You alone, Dwight, are responsible for the fact that the Emory administration asked you to resign your chairmanship and leave the school.

Your statement is misleading and impugns my character. While you were department chairman, you had a pattern of pitting one person against another, usually with partially true information. This led to many misunderstandings. Now you are trying the same thing outside the department.... It only takes one remark from a person in your position to create this kind of doubt. This pattern of yours, Dwight, is unacceptable to me, and I will not tolerate it. It has wrought havoc in the lives of others, and I do not intend to let it disrupt my life or my relationships with friends and valued colleagues.

I know you have suffered dreadfully during this entire ordeal. I have heard you say publicly that this has been a time of enormous personal growth for you; I hope this is true, Dwight. Directing blame and retribution toward others for problems you created is wrong and will be even more destructive for you.

Waring mailed this letter plus his 1984 letter, already quoted in the text, to many colleagues across the country.

Waring and everyone, including me, give Cavanagh his due. He achieved good outcomes at Emory. Cavanagh almost single-handedly raised the money for the eye center and saw through its completion. He recruited an outstanding faculty. Cavanagh fought the internal fights at Emory against entrenched interests who felt the eye was just an appendage of the body and certainly did not deserve a building of its own, even if the money was raised by separate efforts. Despite these achievements, Emory accords Cavanagh scant mention in its official history. The Emory Eye Center website's section on the history of the center barely mentions the years of Cavanagh's tenure.

Sargus Houston's blindness imposed limitations on an already simple life. He spent his days listening to television and radio, never leaving home. An article in the *Macon Telegraph and News* described him in 1990, shortly before the last trial ended:

In the meantime, Houston lives just the same as he has since his surgery—dependent on his sister, Rachel Dennis, staying in their tattered Unionville home.... Dressed Tuesday afternoon in a stained white shirt, a thermal T-shirt, and gray pants, Houston didn't seem to mind the stuffy afternoon heat building up in the tiny, brick duplex filled with warm bodies.... When the surgery left him totally disabled, Houston moved in permanently with Dennis. She said he won't go out because, "He can't see nobody, so he don't go see nobody."

Houston won't even go to church with her, she complained.

"I make sure he always be with somebody," said Dennis. "I stay with him all day. The only time I go out is to the grocery store, to church, to the doctor. I gave up my Bible study.

"But as far as giving it up, I don't mind. He is my brother."

Houston's settlement allowed him to buy a new home and live in more luxurious surroundings, but he remained housebound. He died in 1995.

I interviewed Gladys Wilson in 2005. Macular degeneration has claimed the eyesight of her remaining eye, and her hearing has declined. Yet her mind is sharp, and she remembers details of her ordeal as if it were a week ago. She also remembers that many people did not believe her story, did not believe that an Emory doctor would have treated her so, and do not believe her to this day. Her daughter read her a copy of this manuscript, and she was quite grateful that her story was being told. She turned 98 in the spring of 2009 and she remains as alert as ever. When I touched base with her, she repeated her thanks for telling her story, telling me again that many people still don't believe these events happened.

Mattie Sue Brown died in 1998 at the age of 92. I interviewed her son and daughter and they reported that she eventually adjusted to her one-eyed status and retained vision in her good eye.

Drs. Henry Kaplan and Travis Meredith moved to St. Louis in 1988. Kaplan became chairman of the eye department at Washington University, while Meredith joined the private retinal group, members of which were also faculty of the department. Amazingly, Kaplan refused to allow Meredith to join the faculty. The following letter was mailed anonymously to many ophthalmologists around the country, including me.

April 25, 1991

Dear Isaac,

This is in response to your letter of April 5, in which you request a faculty appointment in the Department of Ophthalmology and Visual Sciences of the Washington University School of Medicine for Dr. Travis Meredith.... After careful consideration it is my judgment that Dr. Meredith would not be a suitable candidate for a faculty position in the Department of Ophthalmology and Visual Sciences. Therefore, I unfortunately will not be able to honor your request.

It would have been most useful if you had spoken to me prior to the apparent offer to Dr. Meredith since you are aware that I have known him for over ten years and am quite familiar with his strengths and weaknesses, both professionally and personally. The desire you express in your letter to establish and maintain a collegial, professional relationship would be pursued by seeking advice before tendering an offer of such a nature....

Sincerely,
Hank
Henry J. Kaplan, M.D.
Professor and Chairman

Controversy and lawsuits marked Kaplan's tenure at Washington University. He resigned the chairmanship in 1998.

In 2000 Dr. Kaplan left St. Louis and became chairman of the eye department at the University of Louisville.

Despite Kaplan's rejection of a faculty appointment, Meredith joined the retina group and stayed in St. Louis for a number of years. He is now the chairman of the Department of Ophthalmology at the University of North Carolina.

George Waring remained at Emory until 2004, when he left the faculty to enter private practice in Atlanta.

Dr. John Wright practiced in Atlanta a short while after leaving Emory, then moved to Boston. He now is on the full-time faculty at the University of North Carolina, where Travis Meredith is the chair.

Dr. Bob Allen moved to Virginia, first to Charlottesville and then to Richmond, where he chaired the eye department at the Medical College of Virginia. He died in 2005, too young, at age 54, from the complications of cancer of the eye. Widely loved and respected, he touched many people in ophthalmology. He deserves special credit for his role in this story. He had the courage to leave rather than stay and have his name associated with a program with which he disagreed. He was forthright and honest in his depositions and never stooped to evasions or equivocations. Most importantly, he secured an agreement that the parties would have public disclosure of any settlement in the Houston suit before he would testify. Absent his insistence on this disclosure, the amount of the settlement would have been private as in the other six lawsuits.

President Bill Clinton appointed James Laney to be ambassador to South Korea in 1993. Laney retired from that position in 1997 and returned to Atlanta, where he remains a respected figure.

Charles Hatcher, now retired, served as vice president for Health Affairs until 1996. Emory has honored Dr. Hatcher in many ways, including establishing the Charles Ross Hatcher, Jr. Distinguished Professor of Surgery Award and commissioning a portrait of him. Emory awarded him the Woodruff Medal of Distinction in 2000, the highest award given by the Health Sciences Center. Emory credits Hatcher with the "unparalleled growth" of the Health Sciences Center and warmly regards his tenure as leader.

Hatcher later settled William Biggers' lawsuit, but the terms were not filed with the court. Later depositions would attempt, unsuccessfully, to learn if Emory paid the legal fees and settlement monies of this lawsuit, since it was against Hatcher personally. His million-dollar-plus salary continued until the late 1980s, and further information is not available.

Emory added an aggrieved patient, Charles Harper, as an "intervener" in the Switz suit. She in turn sued Harper and Emory. Emory settled this suit, which had fizzled, in 1988, with a payment to Switz and a public apology.

Dr. Z has declined to identify him or herself. I know little of Z, but it is likely that Z and Johnny Anonymous are the same person. Certainly, one or more insiders were working to bring Cavanagh down, and working *sub rosa* while David Campbell was working in the open. I believe David Campbell was not Z, but undoubtedly many of the Emory hierarchy did. Z's activities helped lead to Campbell's reprimand, since going outside the chain of command was one of the complaints against David. I feel quite sure that I talked with Z during the course of my research for this book, but I made it clear to everyone that I did not want to know Z's identity unless I could use the identity publicly. No one has come forth.

In the summer of 2008, I called Dwight Cavanagh, Travis Meredith, Henry Kaplan, Charles Hatcher, and Jim Laney, informing each of the forthcoming publication of this book and offering them the opportunity to make comments or share reflections of these days. None chose to comment.

These events happened over twenty years ago at an institution that has changed significantly. Emory is an excellent and well-respected center. Then why write this book? I wanted to document in full detail what happens when leadership fails to respond to people bringing credible warnings about existing problems. The events described here could happen at any university or in any company, public or private. The current headlines bear witness to the many consequences of other leaders ignoring warnings of problems similar to those in this book.

So what should be done? How can a leader winnow out the significant problems from the many issues he or she hears about every day? How should investigations of such problems proceed? How do you balance lapses of judgment and character with the many positive attributes of a person? When do you decide that the bad outweighs the good and someone has to go? What if you're low on the pecking order and see problems? How do you report wrongdoing?

I welcome emails from my readers and will discuss the responses on my website, www.tomharbin.com. I will do my best to respond to each email, but please understand that the potential volume of emails may prohibit me from doing so.

ACKNOWLEDGMENTS

Every author needs help, and a first-time author needs even more than a veteran. Many people gave feedback, encouragement, interviews, access to documents, and other kinds of support.

E. Louie Crew, my high school English teacher, spread the writing seed on very thin and rocky soil when he bludgeoned me and our class into themes, essays, book reviews, and other forms of writing. Those seeds germinated very slowly and finally bore fruit just a few years ago when I began this book.

I relied heavily on documents throughout the book, and many came from the office of Taylor Jones. Many thanks to Taylor and Carolyn Robinson, his assistant. David Campbell and Allen Gammon supplied copies of depositions as well as transcripts of their personal notes and recordings of meetings. Most of all, they offered support, encouragement, and personal anecdotes.

Interviews with former dean James Glenn, Frank and Cathy Bell, Mary Gemmill, Genevieve Switz, Charles Seabrook, and Gladys Wilson provided details that fleshed out the written sources. A few interviewees wished to remain anonymous. You know who you are, and I appreciate your help.

Many people read the manuscript in various stages and versions, offering not only good advice about the writing but encouragement to continue. Thank you to the following: Adam Cole, Robin Cook, Sandra King Conroy, Allen Gammon, Annie Gammon, Mary Gemmill, Bob Harbin, Frank Harbin, Henry Harbin, Bob Hicks, David Hill, Bill Jarrett, Ed Lovern, Jon Lowe, Kris Morrill, Hod Nalle, Allyce North, George Spaeth, Mary Rose Taylor, Linda Tucker, Martin Wand, Bill Waters, and Charlie and Melody Wickliffe. Michael McDonald encouraged my efforts and helped with the title. My writers' group, Joe Baird, Steve Clay, and John Crawford made excellent suggestions for the near-final version.

Sally Brady, first my editor and then my agent, tireless and energetic in both roles, greatly improved my book, and I feel extreme gratitude for her efforts. She made me a better writer.

Finally, a word of thanks to my wonderful wife Ellen, who put up with my early hours and weekend labors. Out of concern for the feelings of our friends from Emory and Johns Hopkins, she offered valuable suggestions for the final version of the manuscript.

PARTICIPANTS

» Hunter Allen: Attorney for Emory Clinic

» Robert Allen: Emory ophthalmology faculty, glaucoma

» Frank Bell: Emory ophthalmology faculty, retina, 1974–1978

» William Biggers: Emory faculty, psychiatry

» Mattie Sue Brown: Patient of Dwight Cavanagh

» Phinizy Calhoun: Emory ophthalmology chairman, retired 1978

» David Campbell: Emory ophthalmology faculty, glaucoma

» Dwight Cavanagh: Emory ophthalmology chairman, 1978–1987

» William Coles: Emory ophthalmology faculty

» Dorothy Fuller: Sargus Houston's sister

» Allen Gammon: Emory ophthalmology faculty, pediatrics

» Mary Gemmill: Emory ophthalmology ophthalmic technologist

» James Glenn: Emory University School of Medicine dean, 1980–1983

» Charles Hatcher: CEO of Emory Clinic until 1983, then vice president of Health Affairs and CFO of Emory Clinic

» Garland Herndon: Vice president of Health Affairs until 1983

» Sargus Houston: Patient of Dwight Cavanagh, wrong eye operated upon

» Taylor Jones: Atlanta attorney for Sargus Houston

» Henry Kaplan: Emory ophthalmology faculty, retina

» Alan Kozarsky: Cornea fellow, then faculty at Emory

» James Laney: President of Emory

» J.O. Martin: Sargus Houston's ophthalmologist in Macon

» James McCulley: Chairman of ophthalmology at University of Texas, Southwestern, Dallas

» Travis Meredith: Emory ophthalmology faculty, retina

» Philip Newman: Cornea fellow at Emory

» Garland Perdue: CEO of Emory Clinic, succeeding Charles Hatcher

» Charles Seabrook: Reporter at *Atlanta Journal-Constitution*

» George Spaeth: Member of ethics committee, American Academy of Ophthalmology

» Robert Spector: Emory ophthalmology faculty, neuro ophthalmology

» Penn Spell: David Campbell's attorney

» Irving Staley: Member of Georgia's Composite State Board of Medical Examiners

» Frankie Stegall: Emory ophthalmology faculty, orthoptist

» Genevieve Switz: Dwight Cavanagh's physician assistant

» Doyle Stulting: Cornea fellow at Emory, then faculty

» George Tindall: Chair of Emory's Neurosurgery Department and chair of Emory's ethics committee

» Roy Townsend: Executive director, Emory Clinic

» George Waring: Emory ophthalmology faculty, cornea

» Gladys Wilson: Patient of Dwight Cavanagh

» Louis Wilson: Emory ophthalmology faculty, cornea

» John Wright: Emory ophthalmology faculty, pathology and pediatrics

APPENDIX:
SOURCES AND BIBLIOGRAPHY

Lawsuits, original and later amended, with attendant depositions, provide many of the details of this book. These suits are listed below, in alphabetical order of the last name of the plaintiff. Other documents include letters, affidavits, transcripts of committee meetings, meetings between individuals, and personal notes dictated contemporaneously.

LAWSUITS

» Biggers, William v. Hatcher: W. H. Biggers, Plaintiff vs. C. R. Hatcher, Defendant. In the Superior Court of DeKalb County, State of Georgia. Civil Action no. 85-8735-5

» Brown, Mattie Sue v. Cavanagh: Mrs. Mattie S Brown, Plaintiff vs. Harrison Dwight Cavanagh, M.D.; Emory Clinic, a partnership, and Emory University, d/b/a Emory Hospital, defendants. In the United States District Court for the Northern District of Georgia, Atlanta Division. Civil Action no. C86-2086A

» Campbell, David v. Cavanagh: David G. Campbell, M.D., Plaintiff vs. Emory Clinic, H.D. Cavanagh, M.D., Emory University and Charles R. Hatcher, M.D., Defendants. In the United States District Court for the Northern District of Georgia, Atlanta Division. Civil Action no. 1:91-CV-1403-HTW

» Craft v Cavanagh: Susan L. Craft, Plaintiff, vs. Harrison D. Cavanagh, M.D.; Emory Clinic, a Partnership, and Emory

University, d/b/a Emory Hospital, Defendants. In the United States District Court for the Northern District of Georgia, Atlanta Division. Civil Action no. C86-2562A

» Emory University Clinic v. Switz: The Emory University Clinic, Plaintiff v. Genevieve Switz, Defendant. In the Superior Court of DeKalb County, Civil Action no. 86-4109-6

» Gammon v. Cavanagh: J. Allen Gammon, M.D., Plaintiff vs. Emory Clinic, a Partnership, Emory University, H.D. Cavanagh, M.D., and C.R. Hatcher, M.D., Defendants. In the United States District Court for the Northern District of Georgia, Atlanta Division. Civil Action no 1:91-CV-3030-HTW

» Hale, Fleischman, and Murphy v. Washington University and School of Medicine: Cynthia Hale, Gerri Fleishman, and Gale Murphy, Plaintiffs v. Washington University and Washington University School of Medicine, Defendants. United States District Court, Eastern District of Missouri, Eastern Division. Case No. 4:98CV02081CAS

» Harris, Reid v. Cavanagh: Reid W Harris, Plaintiff vs. Harrison Dwight Cavanagh, M.D., and Emory Clinic and Emory University, d/b/a Emory Hospital, Defendants. In the United States District Court, Northern District of Georgia, Atlanta Division. Civil Action no. C87-1943A

» Houston, Sargus v. Cavanagh: Sargus Houston, Plaintiff vs. Harrison D. Cavanagh, M.D., Emory University, d/b/a Emory University Hospital and Emory Clinic, a Partnership, Defendants. In the State Court for the County of Fulton, State of Georgia, Civil action no. D-17621

» Jasani v Cavanagh- Lawsuit in Washington, DC. No other details available.

» Kaplan, Henry v. Bobrow: Henry J. Kaplan, M.D., Plaintiff vs. James C. Bobrow, M.D., Defendant. In the Circuit Court of the City of St. Louis, State of Missouri. Cause No. 992-7786

» Mincey, Rubin v. Cavanagh: Lillia Mae Mincey and Rubin Mincey, Plaintiffs vs. Harrison Dwight Cavanagh, M.D. and Emory Clinic, Defendants. In the United States District Court, Northern District of Georgia, Atlanta Division. Civil Action no. C87-1372A

» Photogenesis, Inc, v. Kaplan: Photogenesis, Inc. Plaintiff, v. Washington University, Henry Kaplan, M.D., Defendants. In Missouri Circuit Court, Twenty-Second Judicial Circuit, St. Louis City. Cause no 002-00456, Division No. 1

» Tomlinson, Russell v. Cavanagh: Russell A. Tomlinson, Plaintiff vs. Harrison D. Cavanagh, M.D.; Emory Clinic, a Partnership, and Emory University, d/b/a Emory Hospital, Defendants. In the United States District Court for the Northern District of Georgia, Atlanta Division. Civil Action no. C87-640A

» Wilson, Gladys v. Cavanagh: Gladys E. Wilson, Plaintiff vs. Harrison Dwight Cavanagh, M.D., Emory Clinic, A Partnership, and Emory University, d/b/a Emory Hospital. In the United States District Court for the Northern District of Georgia, Atlanta Division. Civil Action no. C86- 705A

LETTERS

Some of the letters listed below have been quoted in the text; the remainder comprised background material.

Hunter Allen
- » 1988 letter from Mr. Allen to Penn Spell and George Waring

Dwight Cavanagh
- » Malpractice for residents to assist in PK
- » 7/31/84 Memo to faculty—life is a journey
- » 9/27/84 letter to cornea faculty
- » 10/9/86 letter to Dean Krause requesting Leave of Absence and resignation,
- » Krause acceptance of above
- » Letter to Nick Davies, disparaging a patient's care at Eye Consultants of Atlanta
- » Memo to faculty re. financial cutbacks
- » Letter to David Campbell regarding his promotion to full professor
- » Letter to Campbell, accepting his resignation
- » 10/85 letter to ophthalmologists around the U.S. regarding his exoneration
- » 1982 letters to George Waring regarding his absence from clinic and surgical volume

David Campbell
- » 7/16/85 to Charles Hatcher
- » 8/6/85 to Charles Hatcher
- » 9/16/85 resignation letter to Dwight Cavanagh
- » 7/11/84 apology to Dwight Cavanagh regarding his remarks at a faculty meeting

> » 4/2/85 letter to Dwight Cavanagh regarding his raise in salary
> » 11/90 letter to attorney James Butler regarding Genevieve Switz
> » 6/91 letter to James Butler regarding joining his and Gammon's suits

Claes Dohlman
> » Letter supporting Dwight Cavanagh

Tom Harbin
> » Letter to David Campbell, 6/87

Charles Hatcher
> » 7/18/85 to Garland Perdue
> » 7/22/85 to David Campbell
> » 7/22/85 to Dean Krause
> »

Taylor Jones
> » 8/21/89 to David Campbell
> » 9/89 to James Butler regarding Alan Kozarsky and Robert Spector

Henry Kaplan
> » 7/24/85 to David Campbell regarding reassignment of Campbell's secretary
> » Undated letter regarding residents too unskilled for vitrectomy procedures
> » 6/91 letter to Isaac Boniuk rejecting Travis Meredith for faculty appointment at Washington University

Dean Krause
> » 9/23/85 to Charles Hatcher

Garland Perdue

- » 3/3/84 Notes to his file re: Sargus Houston
- » 12/17/84 to Louis Wilson
- » 3/85 Notes to file re: ophthalmology
- » 7/25/85 to George Tindall
- » 8/2/85 to George Tindall
- » 9/17/85 to David Campbell, reprimand
- » Late letter to David Campbell, supporting him
- » 4/16/86 memo re called clinic partners meeting

Doyle Stulting

- » 4/86 letter to David Campbell regarding Campbell's treatment of a patient

George Waring

- » Letter to Dwight Cavanagh, 2/24/87
- » Letter (from committee) to Dwight Cavanagh, 12/6/84
- » Letter (from committee) to Charles Hatcher, 12/6/84
- » Letter to Dwight Cavanagh, 12/14/84
- » Letter, never mailed to Hunter Allen, regarding David Campbell
- » 1984 letter regarding formation of his quality committee

Louis Wilson

- » Letter to David Campbell, accepting resignation, 9/18/85

NEWS ARTICLES/RELEASES

Tindall Committee Press Release, 9/10/85

Atlanta Magazine, "Tell Tale Hearts," July 88,
Atlanta Journal-Constitution
>   "Brilliant Emory Eye Surgeon Under Investigation," 8/4/85
>   "Medical Mistakes: A Fact of Life and Death," 2/23/86
>   "Head of Emory Ophthalmology Taking Leave Until Suits Settled," 4/1/86
>   "Doctor Sues Emory Over Resignation: Claims Was Ousted for Whistle-Blowing," 5/2/89
>   "Doctor Sues Emory Over Loss of Job," 9/9/89
>   "Racial Bias Charge Leads to Mistrial," 2/22/90
>   "Surgeon Tried to Cover Up Mistake, Court Told: Doctor Operated on Wrong Eye," 2/27/90
>   "Suit Against Emory Clinic Is Withdrawn: Lawyer Fined for Action in Case Over Eye Surgery," 3/6/90
>   "Plaintiff Ordered to Pay Jury Fees in Aborted Suit," 3/23/90
>   "Settlement Reached in Lawsuit Over Corneal Transplant," 5/3/90
>   "Blind Man Settles for $4 Million: Eye-Surgery Case Ends after Two Aborted Trials," 5/12/90
>   "Doctor Sues Emory, Alleging Fraud," 7/3/90

Fulton County Daily Report
>   "Must Emory Reveal Peer Review Data? Setback for University in Malpractice Case," 12/30/87
>   "Amicus No Friend of Emory? Former Law Dean Represents Former Medical Professor in Cavanagh Case," 5/19/88
>   "Take $1 Million, Please," 9/20/89

» "Claws Bared for Eye Trial: Judge Threatens Jail to Tame Scrapping Counsel," 2/19/90
» "Hoist By His Own Petard? Like a Trigger-Happy Gunslinger at High Noon, Hunter S. Allen, Jr. May Have Shot Himself in the Foot...," 2/27/90
» "And They're Off...," 2/28/90
» "Back to Square One," 3/7/90
» "Judge Accused of Emory Bias," 3/15/90
» "Having His Fill of Etheridge: Jones Too Wants Judge to Recuse," 4/5/90
» "Venue Battles Rage in Emory Case," 4/9/90
» "Etheridge Denies Recusal Request," 4/23/90
» "Emory Eye Case May Be Near a $3 Million-Plus Settlement," 5/8/90
» "Emory Eye Case Settles for $4.24 Million," 5/14/90
» "Emory Plaintiffs Raise the Stakes," 7/6/90
» "Partner in Emory Clinic May Not Sue Clinic for Other Partner's Wrongdoing," 9/2/92

Southern Magazine: "Sargus' Lament," January 1987

Emory Magazine announcing LAW as interim chair, FF14

Emory Magazine on Darsee affair, FF41

Science Magazine on Darsee, US News article, FF24

BIBLIOGRAPHY

Allen, Frederick. *Atlanta Rising: The Invention of an International City, 1946–1996.* Atlanta: Longstreet Press, 1996.

Gulley, F. Stuart. *The Academic President as Moral Leader: James T. Laney at Emory University, 1977–1993.* Macon, GA: Mercer University Press, 2001.

Kastor, John A. *Governance of Teaching Hospitals: Turmoil at Penn and Hopkins.* Baltimore: The Johns Hopkins University Press, 2004.

Martin, John D. and Garland Perdue. *The History of Surgery at Emory University.* Fulton, MO: Ovid Bell Press, 1979.